VANISHING AMERICA

Also by James Conaway

Fiction
The Big Easy
World's End

Nonfiction
Judge: The Life and Times of Leander Perez
The Texans
The Kingdom in the Country
Napa: The Story of an American Eden
Memphis Afternoons
The Smithsonian: 150 Years of Adventure
*America's Library: The Story of the Library of Congress,
    1800–2000*
*The Far Side of Eden: New Money, Old Land,
    and the Battle for Napa Valley*

VANISHING
AMERICA

IN PURSUIT OF OUR
ELUSIVE LANDSCAPES

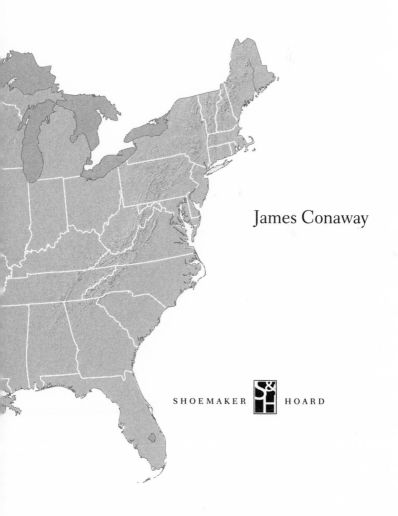

James Conaway

SHOEMAKER HOARD

Portions of this book have previously appeared, in altered form,
in *Preservation, National Geographic Traveler, Smithsonian,
The New Republic,* and *The Washington Post Magazine*. Some
of the names in this book have been changed in order to
preserve privacy.

Library of Congress Cataloging-in-Publication Data
Conaway, James.
Vanishing America : in pursuit of our elusive landscapes /
James Conaway.
p. cm.
ISBN-13: 978-1-59376-128-8
ISBN-10: 1-59376-128-7
1. United States—Description and travel. 2. Conaway,
James—Travel—United States. 3. United States—
History, Local. 4. Landscape changes—United States.
5. Landscape—Social aspects—United States. 6. Landscape
protection—United States. 7. Historic preservation—United
States. 8. Cultural property—Protection—United States.
9. United States—Social conditions—1980- 10. National
characteristics, American. I. Title. 917.3
E169.Z83C66 2007   CON
917.3'0492—dc22   2007010643   11/07

Jacket design by Kimberly Glyder Design
Interior design by David Bullen Design
Printed in the United States of America

Shoemaker **S&H** Hoard
www.shoemakerhoard.com
10 9 8 7 6 5 4 3 2 1

For Penny,

and for Johnny Lang

CONTENTS

The pastoral ideal . . . enabled the nation to continue defining its purpose as the pursuit of rural happiness while devoting itself to productivity, wealth, and power.

LEO MARX, *The Machine in the Garden*

PROLOGUE

For As Long As It Lasts

TROUBLE ARRIVED NOT IN THE GUISE OF A STRANGER, but in that of a neighbor. My wife, Penny, and I had acquired an acre and a half in the shadow of Virginia's Blue Ridge, and the owner of a nearby winery decided to take advantage of a law passed to encourage farming. He would sell raucous events along with his wine, what may seem a small transgression to you, but as anyone who lives in the country knows, everything here is a matter of scale. Thus began a classic land-use fight already too familiar to me as a writer. The conflict would involve meetings and stratagems, testimony before various elected and appointed bodies, and, of course, lawyers.

The serenity and timeless quality of our particular place were threatened even as our social life improved with all the meetings we attended. During that fight—still unresolved—I looked around and saw everywhere fields and structures falling before a procession of would-be property owners much like ourselves: weekenders, city slickers, "cocktail farmers." But many seemed indifferent to the past and hostile to even the smallest sacrifice for the general good, even if gratifying their desires meant wrecking views for others and sullying the way of life that had attracted them in the first place. At one point, I said to Penny, "Let's just enjoy it here for as long as it lasts."

Later, I marveled at how natural those words sounded, and at how readily Americans accept them. If everyone's bit of land is threatened, then so is our collective happiness. Reliance upon permanence is what "home" is about, yet the nation's identity, and much of the ground that manifests it, is being radically transformed by opportunism as we ourselves are by toxic political and social orthodoxies.

The modern conservation movement was born when there was still plenty of intact America to conserve. Back then, the notion that a totality of the natural and the built environments could be changed in a lifetime would have seemed far-fetched. No more. Yet individual concern for the integrity of definitive bits of America is discounted as sentimental or attacked as an obstruction to the overriding quest for material gratification and maximum profits in minimal time.

I HAVE BEEN WRITING about these things in one way or another for years. My interest stemmed from a childhood involvement with the outdoors, once a common American experience but not so today, when products isolate children from unruly nature and leave them with technological addictions and what researchers are now calling natural deficit disorder. That interest was rekindled in my adult years by my close involvement with some of America's phenomenal real estate—the public lands of the intermountain West, including the northern Rockies, the Colorado Plateau, the desert Southwest, and the heavily timbered coasts of California, Oregon, and Washington. There I traveled for half a year in the mid-1980s, talking to people who used these lands, struck by two obvious truths: The seeming inviolability of "protected," iconic landscapes is a myth; and local people's opinions of those places vary as much as any in America and are imbued with all the passion and contradictory beliefs of a historically heterogeneous society.

The land provided a context for debating what the country and its citizenry should be, a volatile argument as old as the republic and farther from resolution than in frontier days. But people had so affected these places in one way or another that they—we—had become essential parts of the landscape. Even de jure wilderness, which had been so declared by the U.S. Congress, reflected the contending desires of human beings, some wanting to keep the land just so in perpetuity, others wanting to capitalize on it by whatever means necessary. Beyond these protected areas were places that had defined themselves decades and even centuries before, and they, too, were becoming obsolete: The physical and spiritual home of the American Indian, and the source of sustenance for countless miners, lumberjacks, fishermen, and farmers, were subject to unprecedented, accelerating change.

Yet these groups' abiding influence on the land was an intrinsic part of it and a marker of American civilization; to lose that to development of one sort or another—malls, McMansions, highways, power lines, gas exploration rigs, and so on—was to be deprived, in perpetuity, of what is arguably the real America. These concerns weren't limited to the West, of course, something that became more obvious to me as soon as I recrossed the Rockies. A new awareness had worked its way into my view of every place I went, from New Orleans to Nantucket, upstate Maine to piedmont Virginia, the lands and the enduring elements of local cultures, physical and social, seemingly as tenuous as the glaciers and traditional livelihoods of the West.

Cultural landscape wasn't a phrase commonly used in the 1980s, but today it's often on the lips of landscape architects, theorists, academics, bureaucrats, and activists. There's a growing interest in keeping not just historic or emblematic structures whole, but also their settings, in an attempt to preserve what's left of the country, whether built or natural. Cultural character is inherent in the whole, the argument goes; even a structure as august and recognized as the U.S. Capitol is seriously diminished by its wrecked surroundings. Yet this realization lags far behind the ongoing impulse to create structural islands of privilege in a discordant terrestrial sea.

Cultural landscapes reflect an activity, or a characteristic, that shaped them historically and are particularly important for that reason; in almost all cases, however, the natural component is essential for the integrity of both place and vision. But the natural aspect is often considered last, or not at all; we speak of "improvements" to land to describe the destruction of its character and the use of concrete and other things to entomb its timeless past. The obvious benefits of nature—repose, familiarity, a vital link between life and livelihood—are increasingly difficult to quantify in a fractured, transient, opportunistic society that demands it.

I began to write about these things in various parts of the country, all components in an ongoing voyage of discovery. Property, I found, and the malleability of communities, was no longer assured anywhere; land in its present state seemed infinitely more valuable to posterity, in a cultural sense, than it would ever again be with those improvements, yet "progress" was still the threadbare justification for nihilistic, temporarily enriching transformations.

Here I bring these pieces together and add new ones, all with the same objective: to assess, for want of a better word, exceptional American places that I think serve as physical and spiritual barometers. Judging by my experience, we're in heavy weather, with more on the way.

Countless other discrete bits of the country would serve as well, but I have chosen the ones in this book because they mean something to me personally and professionally and they provide a mirror of sorts to the writer as well as to the country. All the places in this book have characteristics that I consider unique. I assumed—mistakenly—that they and what they represented would always be there for my and my descendants' inspiration.

Everywhere I travel in America, I encounter a deep sense of loss; Americans have come to believe that growth and entitlement matter more than health and happiness in a country that, paradoxically, diminishes in prospect and comity even as it grows richer. The gap between ideals and means gets larger while access to public institutions—and public land—essential to our identity becomes more difficult. No piece of the nation goes unassigned to market forces. So-called traditional values, including those relating to the earth itself, are altered beyond recognition or swept away.

There is resistance. Many Americans try to live in accord with some notion of decency and permanence, qualities too often at odds with consumption and celebrity, and their stories are here, too. Other Americans hold hard to the old reins of conservation even as the real estate transforms beneath them. Aspects of American life have always been vanishing, of course, but something new is afoot: All the places presented in this book are home to someone, but what is there today may well not be there tomorrow. Such impermanence is one of the worst things that can be said of a society. And all the while, many of the best reflections of what the country once stood for lie around us, abused, exploited, or ignored.

I. OUT WEST

Chapter 1

BIG SUR

Just south of the Carmel River, a field of artichokes ran down to the beach, where surfers risk cold waves heaving against black rocks. Beyond that point, the land shed its California trappings, including Carmel's pastel bungalows, and the continent seemed to tilt upward and to the right. It loomed above us, and the road—named Cabrillo Highway, after one of California's early explorers—became a wrinkle on a steep backside furred with blooming heather. The place was one perpetual edge, I thought, a kind of thumbnail Tibet where ordinary concerns paled before the prospect of gravity and its effects. To live was to cling to the mountain and view things in a vertical perspective that surpassed what was commonly considered beautiful; it was to feel the heat of a persistent sun, to smell eucalyptus and red dust, and to hear—when the wind was right—the reverberation of waves in rocky crypts hundreds of feet below.

It was 1963 and there was no town of Big Sur, just an unincorporated collection of wooden structures that included a gas station, a store, a campground, and a bar or two. Here the Los Padres National Forest, which included much of the Santa Lucia Range, touched the highway. Hairy, bundled figures not yet labeled "countercultural" hooked their thumbs in the clear air, hitchhiking to what I could not imagine, since the next sixty miles of coast looked empty on the map.

Some were bound for Nepenthe's, a bar and restaurant that became somewhat famous when it appeared in *The Sandpiper,* starring Elizabeth Taylor and Richard Burton. But for the moment, Big Sur was not widely celebrated. It languished in a happy sociological trough between the demise of the Beat Generation and the advent of San Francisco's summer of love, which in a few years would bring thousands of day-trippers west for experiences that had nothing to do with literature or nature.

Nepenthe's offered a fine view, as well as black bread and hot soup. The habitués existed on the proceeds of trust funds set up in Eastern cities, according to my friend, another wayward post-grad at Stanford University. They billed themselves as artists, but the real article could be found a mile farther down the road, at the Big Sur Inn, a ramshackle but charming collection of houses up against the mountain. Made of redwood scraps, the cottages had steeply pitched roofs, cunning little balconies, and elaborate, rustic woodwork signifying a highly idiosyncratic intelligence. The inn belonged to an old-timer named Deetjen, a Norwegian emigrant who, according to his story, came south by donkey in the early years of the twentieth century and constructed his bucolic kingdom where the road had then petered out. After Deetjen's wife died, he gathered round him enough legends and compliant young visionaries to keep the beds made, the pancakes flipped, and an occasional fire in the hearth.

The tiny bar supported the elbows of various people wrapped in serapes and animal skins, with staffs and bongs, big silver earrings and beards of fierce impenetrability. Deetjen drank jug wine and, trailed by his cats, wandered around the place sufficiently drunk to be sociable, if that is the right word. He managed to be contemptuous and friendly at the same time, no small accomplishment. He told us he had not spoken a word in Norway until he was sixteen years old, for the simple reason that he had not until that time met anyone he considered worth talking to.

We slept in a tent and hung out at the inn during the evenings, eager for tales of early derring-do in the literary wilds of Big Sur. Deetjen would stare at us, blinking his red-rimmed eyes, and then declare in his thick Nordic accent, "You are dualists. *I* am a monist."

It was all marvelously arcane and *authentic,* and,

besides, the girls serving hot tea and Paisano had about them the woolly concupiscence of apprenticed dharma bums, or so we imagined. We went for a walk with one of them, our breaths freezing in the winter night, our soulful conversation overwhelmed by the intensity of a sky like stretched black plastic riddled with an infinity of bright punctures. The moon broke free of the mountains, spreading a silver film over the broad Pacific, and we had the distinct impression that we could reach out and touch Japan.

Deetjen claimed to disapprove of Henry Miller. That had not prevented the two of them from having long, contentious conversations when Miller lived a few miles down the coast and hiked or rode up to the inn of a long evening. Miller was famous by then, and once the cook sneaked a microphone behind a drapery next to their table, hoping to preserve the spilled wisdom of the two boozy individualists. Deetjen was proud of the association, despite the name he often used for Miller: "guttersnipe."

One night Deetjen insisted that we accompany him to his little house across the courtyard so that he could show us a Miller relic. In fact, we had to carry him. His place was a mess, crowded with books, photographs, empty wine jugs, implements out of his Californian and Scandinavian pasts—and cats. Deetjen revived long enough to claw around the shelves until he found one of Miller's books. Miller's inscription to Deetjen was long and inspired and referred to him affectionately as "a wild man."

By day we hiked in Partington Canyon, to the south, where a fast stream descended through redwoods to the ocean, in a cove where dramatic rocky overhangs, twisted madrone trees, and drifting spray created the visual patina of an Oriental scroll. We waded the creek and found an old tunnel dug through the mountain. The tunnel was full of puddles and broken supports and opened up onto a secret harbor choked with kelp. Waves rolled in with fearsome power, smashing against the rocks and raising the water level fifteen feet in an instant.

An iron cable, snarled and rusted, had once stretched across the harbor's mouth between bleached wooden bulwarks—a testament to what we were sure had been an illegal port for coolies, opium, and timber. More likely, tanbark had made its way down off the mountains and through the narrow passage to waiting ships. Before the invention of chemicals for tanning hides, the bark of the tan oak tree had created a heady industry in the Northwest and wiped out a lot of forest in the process. Remote Big Sur still had its share of tanbark trees, which were protected by the inhospitable coast.

A scramble round the rocky headland provided access, at some risk, to tidal pools full of scarlet starfish. I will never forget the sight of an otter floating on its back in the ocean, eating abalone, blissfully indifferent to the human presence. The isolated stretch further revealed a cave that had been used by coastal tribes a thousand years before. Still full of old oyster shells and blackened by smoke, the cave was, we discovered, occupied by a young man from New York. His girlfriend lived in a shack up the canyon, he told us. When we asked where he really lived, he pointed to his head. "In here."

The canyon above the highway rose steeply beneath an increasingly dense redwood canopy. Generations of needles packed the narrow path above the rushing water and the decaying logging camp. I had never stood directly beneath a redwood, and looking up, I was mesmerized by the loss of depth perception. Big band-tailed pigeons streaked across the thin slivers of sunlight. Beyond the treetops, far up the mountain, precipitous grassy bluffs spread skyward, seemingly inaccessible and infused with mystery. In such a setting, it was easy to imagine Spanish expeditionary forces sailing north from Mexico at the outset of the seventeenth century. One of their leaders, Sebastián Vizcaíno, swept into the big bay to the north and named it Monterey, after the viceroy of Mexico, the Count of Monte Rey. Vizcaíno named these wilds below the bay *Pais al Sur*—country to the south.

A Franciscan mission was established in Monterey in 1770, but the country to the south remained wild for more than a century. Vast ranches were established along what became known as the Big Sur and Little Sur rivers, but a real road did not run the length of the coast until the mid-1930s. Twenty years in the making, the road became California's first scenic highway; the bridge over Bixby Creek—260 feet above the water—remains one of the highest highway spans in the world.

I CAME BACK to the Big Sur the next spring with a beautiful girl I had met in Palo Alto. Her name was Penny. We had a drink at the Big Sur Inn but didn't tarry; I was in love and no longer much interested in the tall tales of a smoldering Norwegian. We camped in Partington Canyon and climbed out onto the rocks, held hands, and watched the gray whales migrating south. They rose and fell like great ships, so close that we could see the spots on their hides and clearly hear them gasping.

The next day, we packed a lunch and scaled those heathery slopes. The magnitude of the hike is difficult to imagine; I am still amazed that we made it. At one point, we turned around, confronted the unblinking blue eye of the Pacific, and instinctively sat down to avoid falling off the mountain.

We discovered—everything was a discovery—an empty house with tin walls, a neglected asset of the rarely used Julia Pfeiffer Burns State Park. It didn't compare with the subsequent discovery, higher up, off state land, of an old shakes-covered cottage with an overgrown grape arbor leaning into the mountain and a hoe rusting in the sun. All we could do was stand and stare at the forty miles of coastline: To the south, huge headlands tumbled into the sea. Heavy timber clung to the creases and the ridgeline, and the bluffs seemed to glow in the midday light.

We knocked on the door of the cottage, but it had been long deserted; faded café curtains covered the windows. The place needed some sympathetic soul to reclaim it, and we talked about doing just that—then, and after we were married, but there were other ambitions to follow.

I OFTEN THOUGHT about that cottage 2,500 feet above the Pacific, and wondered what had become of it. Twenty years later, I found myself in California again, on a magazine assignment. I decided to go back to Big Sur. I expected it to resemble Carmel now and was pleasantly surprised to find the village still unincorporated and the hillsides little populated. There were more people living up in the canyons, but the precious feeling of isolation had endured. The bartender at Nepenthe's told me that Big Sur had become middle class, social protest and free love having been replaced by bowling at the Naval Station at Point Sur. Drinking and drugs were still popular, she added, with chardonnay edging out the jugs, and cocaine replacing pot as the substance of choice. A new restaurant had opened to meet increased culinary demands. It was owned by a man who once a week put his television set and some popcorn into his Volvo station wagon and drove north with his wife until they could pick up a favorite television show beamed through a break in the mountains.

Old Deetjen had died in the interim; his inn was managed by a friend who built fires under Henry Miller's old bathtub and allowed guests to stew in it. The place was as dilapidated as ever. I slept in the cottage called "Chateau Fiasco," with a display of Hindu bells and an amulet tacked to the wall outside. In a guest book on the table, a guest had written: "The raccoon in the room at 3 A.M. was quite a surprise, but fortunate in that it woke me up in time to go to Esalen."

A well-known local painter, Emil White, had opened the Henry Miller Memorial Library in his home down the road. White had grown old in the shadow of those redwoods but had retained a youthful accessibility. People of all ages in Big Sur considered him a local treasure, with justification. White had established the library because he missed Miller and wanted people to have access to his works and to old photographs reflecting the Big Sur of half a century before.

I drove to Partington Canyon and walked down to the ocean. The tunnel through the mountain had been shored up, a footbridge set across the stream, a fence built to prevent people from rock-scrambling. But otherwise, the scene remained unchanged. I hiked up the canyon and then climbed the steep trail I knew would lead to the abandoned cottage, envisioning a collapsed ruin, or the victim of one of the fires that regularly swept the coast range. I heard a chainsaw. From the forest, I could see a bearded young man burning brush near the house, which had a new roof. I could see beet tops in the vegetable garden and beehives on the far slope.

I approached the house, watched by a pair of slate-blue eyes under the bill of a baseball cap held together with baling wire. He wore a ragged T-shirt and work boots, and his expression was neither encouraging nor hostile. I explained why I was trespassing after two decades of curiosity. Instead of ordering me to go back where I had come from, he said, "Let's take a break."

We sat in the yard and talked. His name was Jeff, and he had stumbled upon the place in 1971, eight years after Penny and I had done the same, and decided he was going to live there. His determination had proven to be much stronger than mine. Over the years, he had worked as a journalist and for the U.S. Forest Service, until the house and the one hundred acres came on the market. The property had been homesteaded by a Danish couple back in the 1920s, he said, and later passed to an aspiring developer who fortunately failed to come up with a method of levitating tourists. Jeff put together a syndicate of friends and family to buy it, and he lived on there alone, supporting himself by running occasional pack trips in the remoter parts of the Los Padres National Forest, over the eastern ridge.

"Everything I accumulated in life has finally come to rest here," he said. That included a good naturalist's library, some American Indian artifacts, and a CB radio powered by flashlight batteries. Also a burro and a horse happily stamping their feet in the barn farther up the hill, prospering grapevines and fruit trees, canned food in the root cellar, and the joy of waking up every morning in that setting. We shared his bread and spring water, my oranges and chocolate, and the view I remembered so well. "It's the nicest spot in California," and I wanted to say, the nicest anywhere.

A FEW MORE YEARS passed. One summer I drove to California from Washington, D.C., in a few feverish days. My son, Brennan, grown now, was a student there, and we found ourselves together on the road leading south from Carmel. His long, tousled hair and disdain for sartorial niceties reminded me of people I had seen in Big Sur twenty-five years before. It gave me pleasure and a renewed sense of awareness to see Brennan's reactions to the same things that had originally struck me with such force—the breathtaking drop from the highway's edge, the stands of redwood, and the tidal pools of Partington Canyon. At one point he said, "I think I might bring a friend here. A female type."

We hiked up the mountain the following day, packing fruit and a bottle of Napa cabernet for Jeff. He came warily out of the cottage in cutoff sweatpants. He had, after all, chosen to live there because he valued privacy, and I felt uneasy introducing him to Brennan with a bit of high-country formality that seemed to amuse them both.

Jeff showed us the new vines that he had planted and a fire lane that had been cut through the property since I was last there. The lane had miraculously saved the house from the most intense flames in fifty years. We drank the wine on his little patio, our eyes straying continually to the view. One of Jeff's neighbors from the other side of the canyon dropped by—a mere four-hour detour. I heard Jeff mutter, "Grand Central Station." When the neighbor had gone, Jeff served Brennan and me borscht made from his own beets, and waved good-bye before heading up to muck out the stable.

We slept in a high meadow that night, on the edge of the world. The next morning, a peregrine falcon floated by us in a dream of feathered symmetry and high evolutionary art, its lustrous black eye passing over us in a brief assessment before it dropped from sight. We hiked on down and found a late breakfast under way at the Big Sur Inn. It had come under yet another management. The loquacious Georgian was gone; the ghost of Deetjen had been thoroughly exorcised, and weekenders from Los Angeles and San Francisco in pressed jeans and bright sweaters filled the dining rooms. "This place has been yuppified," I complained, and Brennan smiled.

He could have said then that the trend was upward. Now Big Sur has a "country inn resort" high above the road with a paneled lobby heavy with rustic furniture, lighted footpaths, hammocks strung under shade trees, and in the rooms latticed shutters opening on to a view of high meadows and ocean. There are fires laid, beds big enough for three, matching drapes and throw pillows, and chardonnay in ice buckets. The receptionist was previously a "work-scholar" at Esalen ten miles down the road and into deep-tissue massage, "cranial work," acupuncture, acupressure, rolfing, and "zero-balancing, which is communicating with energy. No hippies now. It's all corporate."

The dirt road behind the inn winds upward through strands of madrone and fir. After half an hour's climb, you can see Point Sur to the north and blond meadows all around, and not a human being in sight, although there are houses now with chameleon roofs blending into scrub and stone. The old elevation of mood still resides in this view and in this air, but the panoramic zero-balancing entails more elegy than discovery.

Lunch is served on the inn's broad deck. On the back of the menu is a promotional paean conflating a love of nature with commercial opportunity: "I am the Hawk. I have sailed the winds over the peaks and canyons, forests and meadows, sea-worn shores and soaring cliffs. This is a land majestic to the eye and the heart, but sternly unforgiving to those who would seek to diminish its primal authority."

Chapter 2

THE ARIZONA STRIP

I WENT TO SOUTHERN UTAH LOOKING FOR A COWBOY
I will call Jacob Hale. I arrived before dawn, expecting
to find him living on an isolated ranch, not in a bungalow in St. George, behind a motel and across the street
from the local mortuary. We shook hands in the glow
of a streetlamp; he reminded me of someone about to
go bass fishing, in boots and Stetson. My rationale for
being there was simple enough: If the cowboy is the
most enduring of Western myths, why not spend time
with one in some of the West's most difficult terrain?

"We're gonna brand down at the watering," he said, a

thick, purposeful, slow-talking man with squinty folds in the downstream corners of his blue eyes. His wife, still in her bathrobe, was loading sandwiches into an ice chest. She said hello, taking the stranger's measure as, I assumed, any prudent frontier woman might.

Their three grown sons and one grandson arrived, reluctant family participants in a male family outing. They loaded two big cattle trucks parked behind the house with saddles and bridles from a jungle of tack stored in the garage with the lawn mower. In went branding irons, dehorners, a butane tank and burner, big syringes, and cans of chemicals for killing grubs living in bovine hides. Working in shirtsleeves in the cold, gelid air, the men were warmed, I suspected, by the certain knowledge of how hot it would get.

We rode out to their corrals on the edge of town, with a view of new condominiums in the rising sun. I had sought out Jacob Hale to discover how ranching was done where there was little or no water. I had not expected him to be a Mormon—the second surprise—and felt foolish because of that oversight. The sons were cordial but not too friendly. We put hackamores with candy-stripe leads on the horses—three bays, a palomino, an Appaloosa brought along by a prospective seller, and two grays—and loaded them. The Hale caravan contained no thermoses of coffee, no beer, no cigarettes or Copenhagen, just a water jug wrapped in wet burlap, and packs of Doublemint on Jacob's dusty dash. "I get the boys to help," he said, driving south. "It's too much work for a man or two. I say that, but in my granddad's day, they packed in for a couple of months at a time, building fires and branding as they went."

Morning illuminated loaflike gypsum buttes, with huge country lurking beyond. This was the fabled Arizona Strip, cut off from southern access by the millennial crack of the Grand Canyon, full of natural disasters and as rich in prehistory as in geological paradox, supposedly an enduring bastion of essential Western values. Plateaus marched off to the east, mythic players in the grander production of the Colorado Plateau. There were only two blacktop—"oiled"—roads on the Strip, a few satellite Mormon communities, and 3 million acres belonging to the Bureau of Land Management (BLM) and the Forest Service, administered from St. George. Some of the land was so arid that a whole section (640 acres) was needed to feed one cow for six months. The area also supported an unusually large version of the mule deer, black-tailed jackrabbits, desert bighorn, mountain lion, the Great Basin spadefoot toad, Gila monsters, assorted lizards and rats, and the desert tortoise.

Jacob had worked the ranch for thirty-five years. During that time, he had taken two vacations, one to upper New York State, the other to Hawaii, and he had not cared for either. Sometimes, he said, he and his wife took a couple of days off and drove to a cattlemen's do in Salt Lake or Grand Junction. Two years before, he had flown back and forth across the Strip in high winds with other members of the BLM grazing district advisory board and two environmentalists, looking at some of the roughest country on earth to decide what might go into wilderness and what might not. That was a kind of vacation.

Each truck raised its own dust typhoon. Three men

and three horses disembarked in the shadow of a butte and headed off in search of calves; the rest of us traveled on toward Wolf Nob. Jacob backed the truck up to a dozer slash, and the horses trotted out. They nibbled at cheat grass while the saddles were applied. "Get your damn head up," Jacob said, chucking his horse under the chin with a boot toe. Swearing, he said, was his only vice.

He never *told* anyone what to do. "I'd just leave that truck there," he said to Bob, his oldest son. He handed me a pair of hundred-year-old spurs that had belonged to his grandfather. "I'd use these to get that bay moving."

I climbed eagerly aboard. Roundups were the stuff of Saturday afternoon matinees—a living relic. Most American beef was raised in feedlots, but a lot of American breeding stock ran on the public range and amounted to a diffuse national treasure in cattlemen's eyes. Four cows stood beyond the draw, with their calves, watching us. "I'd just trail that bunch across the road," Jacob said, and left us.

Bob and I made an odd wrangling team—an Eastern writer and a Western real estate appraiser. He slumped in the saddle, his hat pulled low to block the angling but already hot sun. "I don't like to work at something for nothing," he said of cow punching, and had never considered it a profession. He had been a basketball star in high school. The St. George real estate market, crowded with retirees seeking winter homes, had drawn him in, as it had all the Hale boys.

We moved cows across the road and down the drainage, meeting up with the rest of the outfit. Jacob rode with his grandson, a determined kid in short leather gloves, the fifth generation of Hales on the Strip. "I wouldn't get ahead of a cow," said Jacob, "unless I was trying to head him."

The calves were dragging by the time we came into sight of the corrals. The man with the Appaloosa to sell picked up a particularly runty calf and draped it over his saddle. "Ain't this some horse?" he said. "Only three years old, and he'll let a calf ride. You know he'll pack a deer. Hey, what's that warm runnin' down my leg?" The calf had peed in fright.

A corrugated steel tank sat in the desert, filled by a spring. This was the "watering," not much to look at but the key to the Hales' domain and a star performer in the Shivwits Resource Area. It produced between five and ten gallons a minute, a hidden oasis that supported five pastures—a strange concept in the desert—and three herds. Arizona, like New Mexico, was a water base state. That meant anyone owning a spring, a seep, or a reservoir controlled the land around it in a six-mile radius, even though that land belonged to the government. Jacob's right to the watering was more complicated, however, since much deal making had occurred over the last half-century.

He owned the rights, it turned out, to only three-fifths of two-thirds of the watering, by the sound of it a Gregorian knot that went back to the Taylor Grazing Act of 1934. Then sheep moved across the open range in waves, and herders' camps occupied every butte within ten miles of water. Jacob's father and his partners ran cattle and watered them here and at other springs; when legislation for the Taylor Grazing Act was being discussed, they pooled their money and sent their brightest partner to Washington, D.C. He found out that water meant control, but didn't share that knowledge. Instead, he came back to St. George and began buying up water pockets for himself and thereby the rights to adjoining government land, which was soon strung with barbed wire. The aggrieved partners appealed to the court of the Church of Jesus Christ of Latter-day Saints for recompense. Jacob smiled as he thought about it, looking out over land you had to know to love, home to at least four species of rattlesnake: "I guess he had something going with the bishop."

The lone partner prevailed, only to freeze to death later on Poverty Mountain, propped against a juniper in a blizzard. The partnership dissolved, and Jacob's father ended up with the three-fifths of two-thirds. Grazing allotments are traded on the open market like private real estate. The Hale "ranch" comprised eighty sections, or about fifty thousand acres, of which he actually owned only sixty acres.

The herd went obediently through the gate. We tied the horses to the fence and unloaded the branding gear. The calves had to be separated from the cows, which meant running around and waving, snapping quirts, and shouting. The calves, devoted to their mothers, were quicker than I in dust that was inches thick in the corral and rose in dense clouds. In the excitement, one of the horses reared, breaking a leather strap. Jacob's middle son said angrily, "You'd have thought the last horse to break a sucking bridle would be that ass."

Mormon swearing is carefully proscribed. Satanic references are allowed, but there seemed to be few for the bodily processes, and none for the reproductive one. The word *suck* covers a world of provocation. "You sucker," said Jacob's youngest, of a particularly recalcitrant calf. "I'll break your sucking neck, you little suckhead." He cornered it, but it bolted under his arm. "Why you little . . . sucker!"

We closed the gate, and the excluded cows began to bellow. The butane was fired up and the irons were laid in the long, blue flame. Bob honed his Case on a Kmart stone; the blade was old and thin and very sharp. Castration and earmarks required it, he said. He owned a title company in St. George and at thirty-two had made almost enough money to retire. He planned to buy most of the ranch from his old man, but not as a real moneymaker.

The "sucker" was flipped onto its side and its legs bound with a hank of rope. Middle son took an iron from the flame, red hot, and applied it, leaning into the effort. The calf bawled and lurched as smoke rose from its flank, and the iron came away to reveal a black and greasy brand, the first of several assaults, but by no means the worst.

We all pitched in, grabbing animals and wrestling them to the ground. The bigger ones had to be roped first, and fought. A hoof caught me in the ribs, engendering some respect. I branded some and held calves down for dehorning but drew the line at pressing that hot, circular steel over the nubs of horn. The calves stiffened with pain, frenzied, throwing slobber over their assailants. The nubs fell off, revealing raw pink nerve endings that were then cauterized, producing fresh agony.

Bob did the castrating. Legs widespread, he bent over and massaged the scrotum and in one long, hair-raising wrist pivot lopped it off with his knife and tossed the testicles in the dust. Ordinarily, there would have been dogs there to eat them, or a bucket to collect them for cooking later. Some cowboys roasted them at the ends of baling wire, or fried them in bacon fat, but there were no mountain-oyster fanciers that day.

He cut a plug out of the left ear, an unalterable sign of ownership, and sharpened the knife again with gory hands, squinting in the boiling dust. The calves were branded so they could be identified, deballed so they would fatten up and stay out of trouble, dehorned so they would not injure one another or their handlers, and mutilated so no rustler could alter their identities. Then a needle was shoved through their hides and antibiotics pumped in so they could survive the shock of it all.

At times I couldn't see beyond the current victim. The bawling and bellowing, the men shouting, the roar of the blowtorch, the combined heat of furnace and sun, the acrid smell of burning flesh and hair, the stench of blood and excrement, and the dust became unbearable. Men climbed out of the melee to rest for a minute on the fence, and breathe, before plunging back in. I had attended other roundups and hadn't met anyone who admitted enjoying them. Even the mildest of men and women performed what amounted to calf torture, shutting off some interior mechanism and entering into a brief, savage compact with the animals that drained all those involved.

The last calf, stunned by the ordeal, listed to one side, head and eyelids drooping, dripping blood into the powdered gypsum. The youngest Hale boy said, "You hate to do it. Some of these little guys are only a few days old."

We ate bologna sandwiches, squeezed into the crescent shadow thrown by the water tank. Our grubby fingers left prints in the white bread. The same little calf, I noticed, "mothered up," nuzzling her teats as if nothing had happened.

JACOB DROVE WITH casual regard for ruts and boulders; he had passed over that road thousands of times. Like most ranchers, he spent most of his time in a truck hauling water, feed, horses, and cattle. On a busy day, he would drive two hundred miles, drinking from the jug wrapped in burlap and passing it along. The water tasted of dust that boiled up from the floorboards and blew in the open windows, the only relief from the heat. Dust got into ears and nose and formed little mud deltas at the corners of our eyes. Even the chewing gum was gritty.

"See that mountain over there?" he said. "That was my winter range for nineteen years. I ran a hundred and eighty head and kept records in a little green book. Then the BLM cut my numbers by half. I went over to the office and put the book down on that range con's desk, and said, 'Let's take a ride.' We went up there, and he couldn't find a single place where the range was overgrazed."

Overgrazing had become an academic question here and in most of the West. Plants like sagebrush had taken over years before, when fires were not allowed to burn them off, and woody plants had slowly edged out what grass had not been eaten. Now burning was in fashion again, but there was insufficient understory—grass—to carry the fire over the range. Its growth was glacial where only a few inches of rain fell in a year and in summer the ferocious heat drove the cows to higher, cooler pasture. The water ran into the sand.

A cow needed up to ten gallons of water a day. Twenty years before, the BLM had begun to build the catchment systems—wide dirt aprons in a wash, sprayed with paraffin to make them hold—that channeled rainwater into storage tanks. Although the government paid for them, maintenance was left to the rancher, and even that rankled. Jacob considered the BLM an extension of a generally disastrous American domestic and foreign policy emanating from Washington, staffed locally with some decent people, but rotten at the federal core. "These regulations are destroying us as a country," he said.

I asked if Mormon orthodoxy included unbridled development. He resettled his hat and said, "We believe resources, like everything else, were put here for a man to use. But we have a responsibility to use them wisely. I used to think of myself as an environmentalist, until the movement started. Everything the environmentalists said in the newspapers was so radical." He canceled his subscription to the *Deseret News* for that reason.

His operating costs were too high, he said. ATV drivers out for the weekend liked to shoot holes in his water tanks and sometimes in his cows. The animals were roughly $300 apiece, and it got expensive when they began to die on you. His herd was worth about $200,000, but there was many a slip between the dehorner and the slaughter-house. The falling price of beef was taking ranchers with it. Jacob could lose $200 on a cow he had owned for a year, and a butcher could make $200 in a day cutting up and selling the same animal.

The government helped support a style of life his oldest son was eager to buy in to. But ranchers were not getting rich at public expense. The work was hard, unyielding, often mindless, offering at least the appearance of independence in a time when there was little of that left.

Mormon towns were built like medieval villages, centers of close-knit social and religious life from which radiated paths to useful employment. St. George was a kind of Mormon Palm Springs created long ago against all reason and odds, a triumph of revealed religion over environment; the Strip was part of the commons. "The old-timers built the Hurricane Canal by hand," he said. "Because they couldn't afford gunpowder, they drilled holes and filled them with water, which froze and shattered the rock. You ought to go down and look at it."

Brigham Young kept a winter residence in St. George—a Victorian gingerbread that now attracted tourists. So did the temple rising above what was once desert, a stark, white vision of the church militant in frosted sugar. Jacob's father had looked to it, after a late calling. "He started getting on me about swearing, when of course he had taught me how to swear. He got on me about working Sundays, which of course I did with him most of my life."

Jacob served as an advisor to the bishopric. I asked how he found the time. "I told them there might be a month or a month and a half in the spring and fall when I might not be around. Including Sundays. They said fine, do what you can."

He reviewed applications from Mormons applying for relief from the bishop's storehouse and granary, and put some of them to work on the stake farms, stakes being equivalent to archdioceses. The church was important, he said, but not as important as the family. "We believe in the family and we believe in self-sufficiency. You exhaust the family's resources before you turn to the church."

He was also a member of the church court. A teen-age girl had been excommunicated for premarital sex, he said, after confessing twice; men had been tried for adultery. "The church doesn't try to control people. We believe in free agentry. Without it, the period of trial on earth would have no meaning."

"What about having more than one wife?"

Polygamy meant excommunication, period.

We rode down the main drag of St. George, which was lined with symbols of American consumption—Chevron, Sizzler, Best Western, Montgomery Ward—and loud with the traffic of pickups and customized sedans.

Half of St. George's blond Lotharios had discarded their shirts in celebration of summer. Broad side streets set about with spacious lawns—Mormons were great waterers—crawled with kids on bikes, and a football sailed through a clarity found only in high, arid Western evenings. Parents sat under pecan and mulberry trees, and Jacob's wife was no exception, peeling onions and chatting with her daughter, who had come down from Salt Lake with her husband and children.

Jacob and I unloaded the saddles and tack and drank a Coke in the kitchen, too dirty to be sociable. A plaque on the wall read FAMILIES ARE FOREVER. The house stood on the site of his father's house. "I don't know why you shouldn't have dinner here," he said. "Call me after you get cleaned up."

I checked into the cheap motel next door. The face looking back at me from the bathroom mirror belonged in a Dickensian colliery. I was dead tired and feared I had a broken rib, since it hurt to breathe. I poured dust out of my boots and groped my way into the shower.

Apparently, there was a reason why I shouldn't have dinner at the Hales'. He didn't explain when I called, and so I went up to look at the Hurricane Canal. The suburbs were rife with large, blond young women, about half of them pregnant. They carried small children and gave me and my license plate the cool appraisal I had come to expect. St. George's real estate boom had attracted a lot of outsiders. Even the new faces in church on Sunday were somehow different, Jacob had said—Mormon snowbirds down from Salt Lake for St. George's relatively balmy winters. "I wonder if people here nowadays would undergo what the founders did," he had said. "I don't think so."

An iron fence and well-watered trees surrounded the temple. St. George's burghers with business there straightened their ties in the mirrored glare of their car windows before entering the temple. Some had removed their Stetsons to reveal the rancher's white head and walked oddly in city shoes. I tried to imagine Jacob Hale doing the same. They become something other than cowboys on the other side of the ironwork, but I wasn't sure what.

Only the faithful were allowed inside the temple. Tourists were accommodated in another building, where a recorded voice gave a company version of Mormon history, alternating lights flashing on artists' renditions of the founders. Mormonism grew out of the revivalist fervor of the early nineteenth century in the eastern United States. Its founder, Joseph Smith, Jr., a visionary New York farm boy, supposedly found gold plates bearing the text of Mormon scriptures after digging where an angel named Moroni directed him, and led his faithful west ahead of its prosecutors. After he was martyred by lynchers in Carthage, Illinois, in 1844, Brigham Young took over. The murdering stopped at the Rockies. The recording didn't mention Young's words when he led the faithful into the Salt Lake Valley—"This is the place"— or that the Church of Jesus Christ of Latter-day Saints originally was intended as a sovereign as well as a religious nation.

The Mormons were hated in the West as well. No doubt outfitters, trappers, cowboys, and cavalrymen resented a man having several wives when there weren't enough women to go around and making a go of it in barbarous country by the force of communal life. The United States acquired what was to be Deseret after the war with Mexico; Utah was granted statehood, with monogamy as the condition. The Mormons might have been cultish, but they counteracted some of the excesses that passed for individualism in the West. Deseret—a word coined in the *Book of Mormon,* meaning "honeybee"—became the symbol of the Latter-day Saints (LDS). Bees seemed slovenly compared to Mormons and their accomplishments. These hardworking people had assisted John Wesley Powell in making the first descent of the Colorado River, and they farmed canyon country that even the natives considered uninhabitable.

The temple at St. George was built before the one in Salt Lake City, to bolster flagging colonists who had already made so many sacrifices. Newly married Mormons would travel hundreds of miles over the Honeymoon Trail to get "sealed" for eternity in the temple. The Hurricane Canal was small potatoes compared with the trans-Colorado passage through the Hole in the Rock, when Mormons' wagons climbed onto the plateau over logs driven into the cliff face by LDS men dangling over eternity at the end of ropes. Now Deseret unofficially included Utah, Nevada, northern Arizona, northwest New Mexico, western Colorado, southwest Wyoming, most of Idaho, and the fringes of Oregon and California—an unseen empire that revealed itself in odd ways: the absolute order of cultivated farms and ranches, the tidiness of city streets, that hint of suspicion in otherwise guileless expressions.

Jacob drove far down onto the Strip the next day, looking for strays. He found the water dried up and his cows in yellow mud, bellowing. He would have to come back the next day with a big truck and move them, or they would die. A gangly calf wandered the fence line, and Jacob stopped and put it with three cows before it would mother-up. He didn't get back to St. George that evening until six o'clock, at which point he drove past the house, hit the horn, and continued on to the corrals on the edge of town.

Jacob spread hay for those cows and turned his attention to a tight-bagged one he had milked with difficulty the night before. Her udders were more swollen than ever, blocked by the pressure of the milk. Her calf lay in the dirt, exhausted by the futile effort to feed. Jacob tried to milk the cow into a 7UP bottle, but she lunged from side to side and cut her tail on the barbed wire. He hobbled her, and tried again. Sweat dripped steadily from the brim of his Stetson; dirt caked his face, hands, and boots, and he moved more deliberately than usual. He had been up since four.

He gripped the calf's flanks between his knees and fed it from the bottle. He coaxed it toward the mother's bag. "Other side, babe," he whispered, but the calf still wouldn't nurse.

Jacob pushed him away and began to refill the bottle. Commuters living in the western suburbs and outlying Santa Rosa passed close by, on the far side of a bank of tamarisk; the light on the Frostop restaurant next to the Hale corrals came on. The cow watched Jacob suspiciously, flicked her injured tail, and caught him across the face, splattering him with blood from hat to belt. Jacob said matter-of-factly, "I'll kill you," and went on milking.

The cow lunged, setting him hard against a post. This time, he lost it. "You goddamn hermaphrodite son of a bitch," he said, and hit her over the head with the 7UP bottle. The cow was unfazed, but fresh milk went all over Jacob Hale.

He climbed the fence and walked to his pickup and tossed his hat onto the hood. "Ain't this a hell of a job?" he said, wiping muck from his eyes. "Maybe I can sell this place to Bob and take a day off."

Chapter 3

BISTI

THE WEATHER REPORT SOUNDED LIKE A prescription for the apocalypse: blizzards in the mountains, freezing rain on the slopes, flooding in the valleys, high winds on the mesas, and dust storms on the desert. New Mexico lay in the grip of some strange climatic inversion. Snowflakes the size of silver dollars alternated with gobs of slush exploding against the windshield of the pickup driven by the Bureau of Land Management's paleontologist. I had found him, with some difficulty, because I wanted to know something of the state of the West before the arrival of human beings, and a scientist in the field seemed to be the best, most entertaining way. However, he said, "We're not necessarily going to have a good time today."

He wore a red Phillies baseball cap with nothing to protect his bald head but plastic mesh, bought the summer before in Philadelphia on one of his rare trips back East. The bill cast a shadow over a salt-and-pepper mustache and a determined countenance. Bill—a pseudonym used in another time of retribution against public officials who dared talk to anyone not vetted by their bosses—worked in the Farmington Resource Area. That included part of the Navajo Reservation. Here whites and American Indians lived in a state of perpetual accommodation, but Bill viewed them all as contending primates not nearly as interesting as their antecedents of many millions of years before. The remains of these ancient animals lay scattered throughout the San Juan Basin, and because Bill had once picked up and brushed off some very special fossilized remains, his name rang professional bells.

On a clear day in Farmington, you could see the stacks of the Four Corners Power Plant. We headed south, through the middle Paleocene, past exposed layers of hardened goo full of fossilized nuggets that regularly contributed to paleontological forehead slapping. "We're going to start," Bill said, "seventy or eighty million years ago, when all this was covered by an intracontinental sea."

The San Juan River flowed under natural sandstone pyramids beyond the Lotaburger stand, the health spa, the Navajo Congregational church, and the trailer camp.

The country looked oceanic in the Late Cretaceous. The epeiric sea had withdrawn toward the northeast, leaving mudflats and deltaic swamps thick with creatures out of a nine-year-old's fondest dreams. Now the area was closer to desert, undulating, scrub-ridden. An occasional Navajo hogan squatted in the distance, abandoned for the mobile home set up next door.

We were bound for the Bisti Badlands, a tiny wilderness area recently ordained by Congress. The name was redundant, Bill said, since *Bisti* meant "badland" in Navajo. It comprised only six thousand acres out of a much larger area richly weird in aspect, fecund with fossils. He had shown me one fossil in his office, opening a cardboard box that might have contained chocolates and removing a layer of cotton to reveal a six-inch tooth with a serrated edge, blued by the eons and apparently designed for munching on elephants. "It's too big for *Albertosaurus*," Bill had said. *Albertosaurus* was a forerunner of the greatest carnivore ever, *Tyrannosaurus rex*. "I think it's a T. rex, but don't write that. It'll just start a fight. There's not supposed to be any T. rex in New Mexico."

New Mexico was so lush with fossils that early in the century, scientists from the East and Europe carted home whole skeletons, like paleontological Elgin marbles. But T. rex was academically confined to Wyoming and the Lance Formation—one of many layers of rock and sand. Reputations were built upon that supposition, and the discovery of T. rex in the Farmington Resource Area was downright incendiary.

The Bisti dropped away to the east, a wasteland of

earthen mushrooms with sandstone caps and dark shale layers in the sides of lunar ravines. Bill and nine other scientists had spent a summer covering four million acres of such country, inventorying dinosaur bones and related occurrences. Their data were instrumental in the argument for wilderness, and in opposition to development of the underlying coal seam, part of the Fruitland Formation—compressed swamps transformed over the millions of years into a commodity that could be easily stripped in the Holocene, that is, the present.

I was surprised to see the Sunbelt Coal Company sitting on the edge of the Bisti. "The boundaries are political," Bill said. "The coal isn't all that good, but the government wants it developed. We're just back from the shore here," he added, a leap of seventy million years, to the epeiric beach. "Animal and plant communities rose all along the emerging shoreline, in broad estuaries and deltaic environments."

A flock of goats and sheep passed in front of us, a Holocenic intrusion, herded by a dog that looked to be half Border collie, half Australian dingo. They were followed by a Navajo on a white nag, the man's parka hood pulled forward against the drizzle. He rode down the hill without recognizing our existence.

The rain was turning the clay surface into organic grease that threatened the efficacy even of our four-wheel drive. We left the truck by a fence and climbed over, onto official wilderness. In Cretaceous times, balmy winds kept the *Hadrosaurus* happy here and warmed the waters where giant sharks and rays nosed about in the mud. A few of the swimmers were covered by it and came down to us in crystallized reproductions, but most fed primordial appetites, or those of erosion—the paleontologist's chief adversary before the invention of bulldozers. "There were turtles," Bill said, picking up a bluish bone chip the size of a nickel, eroded out of a slope. "Lots of turtles. They varied from the size of your hand to that of a tabletop and were important then, as they are now, as good environmental indicators."

It was a great day for sparrow hawks. I had counted twenty-seven sitting on telephone lines like notes in a scale, rising and falling with the wind, or feasting on voles or other creatures emerging from the rarely moist earth. "There were probably lots of birds in the Cretaceous. Bird fossils are almost nonexistent. Their bones are delicate and easily degraded, but we think they were pretty much like our ducks and cranes."

The hawks disappeared as we hiked into the maze of clay canyons. Bits of reddish clinker and jasper-like sediments trailed down the white, fissured banks. They confounded my sense of direction and made walking an exercise in slow motion. Imagine trying to climb mounds of wet, buttered popcorn, littered with bits of petrified wood. "Angiosperms proliferated sometime in here. Hardwood-like trees, and a cross between swamp cedars and something coniferous, with huge buttressing roots so they could stand in the muck."

Bill picked up a piece of rib, thin and crocodilian, prey for serious Cretaceous survivors. Dinosaur bones were considered sacred by the Navajo. Medicine men ground them up and blew the dust into the nostrils of the sick. The early crocodiles are particularly dear to

Bill. While still an undergraduate student of geology at the University of New Mexico at Albuquerque, he used to wander about in the Torrejon Wash, in Sandoval County just south of us. He had the emotional drive of a late arriver on the shores of his chosen discipline, and no money, so he spent his spare time in places most people would not go if paid. One Labor Day, then more than twenty years ago, he noticed something odd protruding from an eroded channel bank or, as Bill later wrote in the *Journal of Paleontology,* "in a gray sandstone lens in the Nacimiento Formation." That is the way he had come to think of geology, not as earth but as a kind of temporal solution in which floated the avatars of his real obsession.

He poked at the protuberance with a chisel. It was a bone, or a collection of them, forming the articulated hind foot and vertebrae of something quite old. He and a companion chiseled off the section of stream bank and loaded it into the car. Bill took it to his apartment and, over the next six months, worked on it—with a toothbrush, a dental pick, and some carbolic acid— removing the sandstone accretion a grain at a time. He knew he was on to something big, but he did not know how big. In the meantime, he attended geology classes and worked as a typist in the department, earning $175 a month, his sole source of income.

Slowly he revealed scales, or scutes, on the foot and spine of the bone he had found, and he found more scutes in the sandstone matrix. The scales bore points not described in any textbook. The Geology Department did not know what to make of them. Bill had met Wann

Langston, an authority on fossil crocodilians, on a field trip, and Langston agreed to become his sponsor. The bones apparently belonged to a new genus and a new species of crocodile, but proving it to the satisfaction of paleontologists was another matter. Ordinarily, no new genus would be accepted without a head, and this creature's head had washed downstream several million years ago. The scutes, however, were perfect and undeniably new, and the find made somewhat famous the finder who five years before had been selling used cars in New Jersey.

THE BISTI is part of a larger chunk of BLM wilderness known as the De-Na-Zin—Navajo for "standing crane." We had to drive in a loop, on a slippery berm passing for a road, to gain access to it. The meteorology was not improving. "This weather pisses me off," Bill said, with a personal antipathy rare in noted scientists. Before coming west, he took an aptitude test, one of those rare alignments of talent and prognostics, and was told that he should be a paleontologist. Rejected by many universities, he was finally accepted by the state of New Mexico, packed all his belongings in two suitcases, and boarded a bus.

"The Bisti has no extreme significance in itself," Bill said, "but it does provide an opportunity to tell the bigger story. During the marine transgression, different formations were laid down, one on top of the other, each more upland." We were covering roughly a million years every fifteen minutes. Miraculously, a van appeared ahead of us, rushing out of the Late Cretaceous; it passed, throwing a tarpaulin of mud across our windshield. Bill stopped and sat cursing, quietly and persistently. "I wish the son of a bitch had gotten stuck, so I could not pull him out."

We took another road that crossed a wash of glistening sand. We got out to inspect. "Quickmud," he said, driving his heel into the stuff; water ran six inches beneath the surface. A BLM pickup had gotten stuck here the year before, and another was sent down from Farmington to pull it out. The second pickup got stuck as well. A tow truck was then dispatched, and it also became stuck. Eventually, a bulldozer hauled them all out, after almost succumbing to the sediments as well. Around the office, they still referred to the episode as the Fifteen-Thousand-Dollar Mud Job.

We backtracked and took yet another road across Split Lip Flats. I was glad for the presence of a radio. We left the truck on the edge of Hunter Wash, overlooking yellow hills that belonged to the Kirtland Formation, and eroded pockets of Ojo Alamo sandstone. It was all part of the same vast drainage, but by now, the Bisti had had its day. "I want you to take a good look at this," Bill said, "because when we get over there, it's going to seem entirely different."

We descended the bank and crossed the wash. "The Kirtland's full of clam beds and mollusks. Pelecypods and brachiopods. There's an upper and a lower Kirtland, paradise for stratigraphers and sedimentologists. We're into a lot of neat things here," he said, and he did not mean the coyote tracks. "Big dinosaurs—*Kritosaurus* and *Parasaurolophus*, both hadrosaurs. Twelve feet tall, with duck bills and hundreds of teeth." Bipedal, semi-aquatic, they ground up vegetation by the wheel-barrow load. *Parasaurolophus* had a hollow horn protruding from its head and through which it may have emitted irresistible love calls.

The hadrosaurs were regularly ground up by teeth similar to the one in Bill's office. A researcher working for Bill had come upon the tooth a mile or so from where we hiked. Bill had found an entire femur weighing four hundred pounds, part of a remarkable food factory that until recently was considered foredoomed. "Dinosaurs lasted one hundred and thirty million years. That's pretty successful."

Bright crimson flowers surrounded a pile of coarse-grained sand—an anthill landscaped with Indian paint-brush. It was a good place to find fossilized fish teeth if you were willing to sift. Water and wind had eroded what once covered layers of prehistory—layers that hung suspended in the present, botanically sterile, intellectually evocative. The Nacimiento Formation sat comfortably on the Kirtland, meaning there was no break between the two periods. The Ojo Alamo, however, sat uncomfortably on the Nacimiento. "Something's missing," Bill said. "We don't know the time hiatus involved. That's the big question."

Faunal changes in the upper Kirtland showed a progression from coastal to upland environment. "You're looking at the end of the dinosaurs and the beginning of the age of mammals. That band of dark rock is the upper limit of the Cretaceous. No dinosaurs meant a chance for great diversification—a lot of job opportunity.

This may come as a surprise to you, but there were small communities of mammals among the dinosaurs, little, primitive, shrewlike things feeding on insects and plant material, maybe on dinosaur eggs. Mammals are my favorite things," he added.

He picked up a handful of flintlike chips. "Calcinated petrified wood. This is a pre-Anasazi lithic area. Early man turned these into projectile points, like chert." He put them back. "I'm on a natural high with this stuff. I go home and I study paleontology. If I worked for a university I would need a Ph.D., which I don't have, and after I wrote the thesis, all this field research would be over."

The government kept him in the field, despite Bill's assessment of the bureau: "The BLM doesn't recognize paleontology. It's unfunded, so they stick it under anthropology. Indirectly, it has to do with man, so it's okay." He laughed. "The politicizing of the Cretaceous."

We mounted into the Ojo Alamo. A petrified tree the size of a sequoia lay along the sandstone spine, soaked by infinite rains, the cellulose replaced by brilliant red jasper and quartz like pure agate. An even larger tree lay below it, downed in the same direction, a good seven feet in diameter at the base. I walked it off: eighty feet of petrified angiosperm with a clean break in the trunk that might have been cut with a chainsaw fifty-eight million years before. "I'd like to know what toppled these mothers," Bill said.

I asked if it could have been the asteroid.

"An asteroid would have had to hit out in the Atlantic. But it would have triggered storms, and floods."

The Rocky Mountain orogeny had already occurred. The big trees lay at the wrong angle to prevailing winds and drainage in that epoch, another surmise that Bill would have to leave untended. We were, I realized, now on the trail of man. It led downstream, toward Angel Peak, where one wing of a natural seraph had been knocked off by an airplane in Recent Time. Bill was looking for evidence of man's immediate predecessors in its shadow, but this would have to wait. "If it gets any wetter, we could be in trouble," he said. "We could be in trouble right now. That road's going to be slick as monkey snot."

Ice crystals had formed on the pickup by the time we reached it, soaked and panting. Bill fought the wheel all the way back to the road. The front end of the truck nosed along in the ditch; the back end kept coming round to meet us. We crawled sideways for thirteen miles, through gathering snow—April in northern New Mexico. "You know," he said after a while, "I would love to have taken a helicopter ride across the San Juan Basin fifty-five million years ago. That would be the greatest trip of all time. But I would like to have lived right here ten thousand years ago. Man was established then; he was dominant."

Chapter 4

THE WYOMING RANGE

THE ROAD RAN DOWN ACROSS CRACKED AND BEDDED lava, gigantic cinder piles with green pastures in the cracks, and a backdrop of thunderheads. I was headed for Wyoming, near the old Oregon Trail, which could still be seen in ghostly meanderings across marginal grassland and broad drainages. It had led prairie schooners down from the Continental Divide, but settlers weren't the only transients around the time of the Civil War. Journalists followed, among them Mark Twain, a prisoner of the overland stage. In 1860, he ate breakfast in Green River and described it in *Roughing It*: "hot biscuits, fresh antelope steaks, and coffee—the only decent meal we tasted between the United States and Great Salt Lake City."

Horace Greeley, the participatory journalist who perfected the newspaper editorial, had passed through a year earlier, after leaving the Great Plains. "I would rather not bore the public with buffalo," he wrote in *An Overland Journey from New York to San Francisco*. (I would later learn that buffalo are anything but boring.) Greeley lost his trunk in the swollen Sweetwater River and got sick from drinking the water, but he had already uttered his famous words, "Go west, young man," to a devout New England Congregationalist in 1854.

Roadkill pulled me up short of Rock Springs. On the edge of the highway lay the head of a cow elk, picked at by a pair of magpies. The birds rose reluctantly, black and white and electric blue, trailing preposterously long tails. The elk's eyes were gone, the neck had been neatly severed, and the mouth hung open, long tongue lolling on the tarmac. Whoever killed it had dressed the animal on the spot and tossed the haunches into their conveyance and the guts into the ditch. This seemed an apt metaphor in the so-called Overthrust Belt, a lapping of tectonic plates deep in the earth. The belt harbored oil and gas and had fostered boom and bust for longer than anyone could remember. Energy exploration and extraction were transforming—and, in the first decade of the twenty-first century, would be wrecking—much of the intermountain west.

Rock Springs looked like a metallic Bedouin encampment in lunar hills, and so I didn't stop. "The only play these days is in sour gas," I had been told earlier by a Chevron executive, "up at Big Piney." *Sour* meant poisonous. The contrast between country and machines seemed starker in Wyoming than in Arizona or New Mexico, the drilling rigs more angular, the billboards higher, the sun fiercer, the wind more capricious. Snow fences line long, straight roads where weirdly jointed transports shuttled high-tech pipe, and there were more severed heads under cottonwoods in the Green River flats, these belonging to sheep. Nothing lasted long around here once it hit the ground.

Big Piney was marked by modular yellow housing units to accommodate thousands of expected workers, but the town did not look ready for prosperity. A couple of bars and motels, a mud slick for a main drag, a water truck holding up traffic, and lots of Texas license plates. The Laundry Basket advertised hot showers for a dollar. I chatted with the proprietor after getting my quarters. There weren't enough bathtubs, or beds, in town, she said. People slept in trailers, vans, cars, even tents, before the sheriff moved them on. She had come from Spearfish, South Dakota, and her husband, a preacher at the Church of God, had a difficult ministry, the bars full every night and men fighting in the mud.

I went into the Silver Spur after my shower, looking for a public telephone. The sun cut meanly through the front window, illuminating old-timers pushing their Coors around in puddles of sweat. Young outsiders with new jobs played pool savagely, cussing and finally hurling their cues onto the torn felt and stalking out to supper. No one paid them the slightest bit of attention. There was no television, no jukebox, and no telephone. A sign above the whiskey supply read, TOWN ORDINANCE, BARROOM FIGHTS $750 AND SIX MONTHS. I ordered a beer.

"You meditatin', or what?"

The question came from a man wearing two hats. The bottom one, a pinched Stetson, might have been used to brew tea. A ball cap from a manufacturer of earth-moving equipment rested on top. He asked what brought me to Big Piney, and when I told him I was a writer, he assumed an expression that was part horror, part hilarity. I asked him what he did for a living. "When I'm not a roughneck, I'm just a sorry-assed cowboy."

When he wasn't either, which was most of the time, he ran errands for the barmaid, hauling beer and ice from the back room, and got free shots of Calvert's blended whiskey in return. I asked why, if Big Piney was booming, the sign outside town said there are only a couple hundred residents. "What do you want 'em to do, go out and change it every day?"

And did he plan to work in the sour gas fields? This, too, offended him. "I've been in the oil patch thirty-five years. I helped build those rigs outside a Casper, where John Wayne filmed *Hellfighters*." He had helped Red Adair put out two big fires on oil rigs. He didn't need sour gas.

"You think this boom will last?" It was the nature of booms, of course, not to.

"You say you're writing a book?" he asked. "You sound stupid to me."

Texans' cars were pulled up outside the rooming house like mullet on a moonlit beach. The sun was just going down. The communal telephone hung on the whitewashed wall, where a Texan stood arguing with his girlfriend in Amarillo. While I waited my turn, a man without a shirt crossed the road. On one side of his chest was tattooed a tropical bird, on the other a rose. He said to the man on the phone, "You gonna buy the fucking thing or git off?"

The Texan got off. I graciously gave up my turn; the man made his call and then shook my hand. "This place is going to hell," he said. "A lot of riffraff coming in."

I called Exxon headquarters to get directions to the development site the next day. The engineer sounded suspicious. Exxon's play in Wyoming was the envy of the other majors, supposedly one of the largest natural gas fields ever developed; there was a lot of money at stake.

THE CONSTRUCTION office sat on a rocky knoll at the end of a long, oiled road that sucked at the tires of speeding pickups. Some workers came as much as a hundred miles each morning and turned around in the afternoon and drove back. The site, most of it Forest Service and Bureau of Land Management land, had the raw, utilitarian look of occupation. The man I was to meet was being briefed on the contingency plan for escaping if a gas leak developed. Hydrogen sulfide—sour gas—smelled like sulfur dioxide but, unfortunately, destroyed the olfactory nerves before you could be sure of what was killing you. A contingency dinner had recently been held at the Pit and Primer in Big Piney for supervisors and their wives, to make sure everyone knew what to do. The gas wells had flags displayed—green, yellow, and red—and a certain combination meant get the hell out.

A small, intense woman sat in the office, under the hierarchical chart for such emergencies, and talked in a low, persistent monotone: "They say there's no danger. If that's true, why do we have all these plans and meetings? Why are we always looking at flags?" She and her husband owned twelve hundred acres just to the north, she said. "It was wilderness—perfect, beautiful. Suddenly we find ourselves surrounded by a sour gas field. They bought our neighbors' land and moved them out of the country. We still run a few cows, but I'm afraid for my children to be there. Exxon has all these evacuation plans, but the local people haven't been told anything. The company's afraid to spook them."

Her husband had given up full-time ranching to work for a pipeline company; she worked for Exxon. "We're all caught up in something bigger; we don't like it, but depend on it. That bothers me a lot."

I found myself in the office of the construction boss, a weight lifter named Mike whose yoked shirt and jeans barely contained 220 pounds of definition. He worked out every evening in the Big Piney high school gym with the head of his team for Quality Assurance, better known as QA. His blue eyes were magnified by contact lenses, and his red hair was carefully swept back. Four pristine Exxon caps—trophies in the oil patch—hung on pegs behind his desk. But he didn't want to talk about sour gas; he wanted to talk about Exxon's proposed reclamation, known as ERRP—Erosion Control, Revegetation and Restoration Plans. "A record amount of money's being spent here. We're gonna reclaim roads, pipe-line segments, well pads. There are plans for each of thirty-nine wells and seventeen gas-gathering segments. We're bringing in aesthetics people, and botanists, to study stream crossings, how to put back topsoil with-out destroying the microorganisms, a lot of stuff." He pointed to a set of plans on the wall. "This little ERRP is a fifteen-million-dollar ERRP. No other oil company would go to these extremes."

His cowboy boots shook the prefab building as he stalked from office to office lining up QA and QC (Quality Control), safety people, and Forest Service and BLM reps for me to talk to. Exxon had invested $3 billion, including the sweetening plant (the process that removed sulfur from the gas) further south, he said, and planned to pour in $5 billion more. The discovery promised to be bigger than Prudhoe Bay; they were talk-ing revenues in the neighborhood of $2 trillion.

Construction went on seven days a week. The federal government's representatives took turns working four days at a stretch, supervising all aspects; the employees overlapped on Wednesdays, so that one person could catch up on what the other had observed Exxon doing on public lands. The Forest Service rep I met wore civil-ian clothes and a Cat hat, an eager part of the team and an unabashed advocate of development. The Forest Service had come a very long way since it considered the national forests preserves. Now its agents looked at color chips so buildings could be painted the same hue as surrounding terrain. Even chain-link fence was color-coordinated. Helium balloons had been flown at the height of prospective drilling rigs, to determine if they were visible over the next ridge.

I got to meet an "aesthetics" person. Exxon's was on loan from an environmental consulting firm in Helena, Montana. He wore lace-up boots and affected a Southern accent to deflect criticism of his modest environmental concerns. "We're into visual resource management," he said. "VRM is looking down a pipeline. If it's not straight, it's less repugnant to passers-by. They're really concerned about that here." He helped Exxon's environmental coordinator. "We come up with some theoretical niceties. My job is to make sure the niceties get put in the minds of the Cat and scraper drivers."

Wyoming's traditional relationship with developers was roughly analogous to that of prostitute and john; most of the state was still spread-eagle. "The oil companies have done what they pleased," he went on. "Here we have a pure strain of Colorado cutthroat trout, elk and moose wintering grounds. A sacred aura. When Exxon says it's gonna put in thirty-nine wells, everybody says, 'Oh, Jesus!' But we haven't had the typical foaming-at-the-mouth environmentalists you have in Jackson."

Exxon had given money to the Big Piney crime task force to handle increases in rapes and battered spouses, and more to the state; the company had bought up ranches along streams to provide anglers with the access they were losing in the sour gas field. Exxon was raising the pipeline above South Beaver Creek to avoid the cutthroat spawn and the fall runs of browns. It had commissioned an elk study—"They paid that ole boy sixty thousand dollars"—and recognized an elk calving "window" between June 15 and July 1, when blasting and other activity ceased in the aspen meadows.

Elk were a big factor in the economy. "Hunting licenses are just like tickets to a circus. To sell more licenses, you need more animals to shoot. That means you need more winter hay and more area for feeding. The state gets a sugar daddy like Exxon to buy more land and forage, and that means more elk to sell more tickets to kill, to raise more money for the state. It's a cynical game," and it was played on federal land.

"You get all these boys out together on site identification. The ID team has somebody from wildlife—bugs and bunnies—aesthetics, soils, veg, Forest, BLM, and basically reaches an accommodation on how it's going to be done. When push comes to shove, it's the twelve and a half percent federal severance tax on a trillion cubic feet of gas. If it's a choice between royalties, and cows and elk, royalties are gonna win. Throw in a little seed, throw in a little environmental mitigation, a little socio-economic mitigation, and everybody goes away happy." But as everyone now knows, many of the royalties due for energy extraction on public lands are never paid.

I drove up to the construction site where lessons were being given in the use of air tanks. An expert in a black jumpsuit stood in the sun and showed the assembled workers how to unpack the tanks from cases and slip on the facemasks. Each worker had to breathe from them for a while to get a sticker for his hard hat. No sticker, no job.

Lights on the rigs would go on at ten parts per million in the atmosphere, the instructor said. Sirens would go on at twenty parts per million. One hundred parts per million would knock you down. It wouldn't kill you outright, but would paralyze your lungs. "Instruction cuts down on lawsuits," he told me later. "They run into millions now. People aren't cheap anymore. Used to be if one kicked off, you'd just go out and hire another 'n."

Anyone who made it this far into the Exxon camp could join the chow line. The woman in front of me had driven all the way from Colorado Springs on chances of finding work. "Only five hundred miles," she added, and a chance to earn minimum wage. I went looking for a tool-pusher, the boss of a drilling rig. I had a map provided at headquarters, but the dirt roads were unmarked and the area of development vast. Soon I was lost, pushed off the road by dump trucks and mesmerized by the country and scale of its transformation: big stands of "quaky" (aspen) where elk calved and some beautiful meadows at close to ten thousand feet. The structures housing equipment had been painted green, and most of the blue steel drilling plants would someday be gone. The roadbeds would be graded and seeded, the whole scene thoroughly ERRPed. But from almost any perspective, the place was, and would remain, a mess, though a color-coordinated one.

THE HUNTING CIRCUS the environmental aesthetician had spoken of was run by the Wyoming Game and Fish Department. The land might belong to the feds, but the animals on it belonged to the state, as did the revenues their killing produced. Blood sport was a strong force for conservation. The name of a biologist, Bruce Johnson, had surfaced in more than one discussion of wildlife—bugs and bunnies. He worked for Wyoming Game and Fish and was the official state representative on teams determining where well pads and roads would be constructed and where mitigation would be conducted.

I called him at home in Big Piney, and the next day met him for some fieldwork near Riley Ridge, close to the Oregon Trail. He looked a decade younger than his thirty-five years, thin as bed slats, with bright blond hair and freckles. He had earned a Ph.D. in biology from Colorado State through his studies of bighorn sheep. "The Wyoming Range is a sacrifice area," he told me right off. "The environmentalists in Jackson have told the developers they can have it as long as they stay down here. South Piney Creek is the Maginot Line. This county is the size of Israel and has only seven thousand people. There's no way development can be legally stopped now. My tack has been to work with the developers as much as possible, to keep the decisions management ones, instead of political."

The sacrifice area, one of the most diverse for bugs and bunnies in the lower forty-eight, wintered thousands of elk and antelope, mule deer, moose, black bear, and bald eagles. Now, in summer, there were sandhill cranes, whooping cranes, and maybe a few endangered black-footed ferrets. We got out of the Game and Fish pickup to do a "pellet group transect," a theoretical elk count based on the frequency of their droppings. Bruce drove a dowel attached to a twelve-foot cord into the ground, and we walked together around the circle, noting the number of fecal groups within its radius. By taking ten such counts, we could sample a tenth of an acre and then extrapolate. At the end of our first circle, he said, "Cows one, elk zero," and wrote on his clipboard.

We continued upslope, counting elk turds. I could feel the systematic assault of seismic blasts over the ridge, as scientists of another sort pursued a regimen just as speculative and a lot more violent. Bruce ignored the blasts. In four years, the elk pellet groups had fallen from thirty to five.

Every year, three thousand hunters came looking for elk. The Forest Service and BLM were still cutting timber, reducing cover, so game was easily seen from the new roads put in by the oil companies. The kill provided another basis for the elk count. Bruce and his colleagues also kept track of the numbers with radio collars attached to a relatively few elk, with elaborate maps tracing the movement of each animal. "Each line ends in a kill site. I use that as a data analysis unit." Aerial counts were done on half-mile grids using several airplanes, one with a computer on board. All the information eventually found its way into a computer model for management by objective. "If we're wrong on our assumptions," he added, "we could be screwing up the whole population."

Elk were gaining on the cows. By the time we finished counting droppings, we had forty-two pellet groups, a slam-dunk victory. "The elk are back right here," said Bruce, "because Exxon has had no activity in this area for a year."

WE LATER WENT jogging on the $275,000 petroleum-base track contributed by Exxon to Big Piney High School. Taxes were ridiculously low in Sublette County, he said, because the energy companies carried so much of the revenue weight. But the cost of living was roughly equivalent of that in Fairbanks. I bought a bottle of Bardolino for double the usual price. Bruce's wife had found a single apple in the supermarket the day before and bought it, only to find it rotten throughout.

Her name was Mary and she made spaghetti sauce from scratch. "We can never find Italian sausage," she said, opening a can of tomato paste in a small kitchen in a small house two blocks from the Silver Spur. A biologist as well, she studied whooping cranes, collecting samples of biota from beaver ponds and other habitat. She had spent six months in Africa, could speak Swahili, and had named their big lab Suki—Swahili for "good fortune." She was studying another African language, Turkana, and the Johnson library was full of books on Africa, including those of Alan Moorehead and Isak Dinesen. "We're considered eccentrics around here," Bruce said, "and we accept that. We don't have as many close friends as we would like, and we can't buy the kinds of food we want, but that's okay."

Because she was pregnant, she drank no alcohol. She was a student of wine, however, in a town where there wasn't much to choose from. She gritted her teeth and passed up the Bardolino during dinner. She and her husband spoke of their common workplace—Riley Ridge—as if it were small and intimate, and theirs. I had the feeling they shared something unquantifiable, a kind of spiritual proximity, although they were usually separated by a couple of ridges and a lot of country. Both were looking hard for finite means of solving difficult, maybe hopeless questions. The fauna demanded the same approach here as in Africa. In the case of human beings, the cultures were behavioral: The Africans were devoted to cows, the Exxon engineers to sour gas. In both cases, reality had to be put through filters, and actual accomplishment was hard to measure.

I asked what they wanted to do most.

"To start a wildlife park in Kenya," she said.

"You need to have a few dreams," said Bruce.

THE NEXT MORNING, we returned to Riley Ridge. Bruce was part of the interdisciplinary team working on a proposed well site. The problem was not visual, but environmental; elk used it for calving, and Bruce had to go head-to-head with the engineers to keep them from ruining it.

The dirt road was lined with pickups. "That's the standard pose of an Exxon man," Bruce said, pointing to one, "standing in the door of his pickup with a phone to his ear." There were in fact four Exxon men present, plus environmental consultants flown in from Helena, from the same consulting firm that the aesthetician worked for. They were hired specialists in soils, vegetation, hydrology, bugs and bunnies, and aesthetics. Also BLM and Forest Service reps, milling around their Suburbans.

We all struck out through the woods. "The decision

has already been made to put a well here," Bruce said. "Exxon's just got all these people out here to wander around and play the game." The National Environmental Policy Act required such collective scrutiny of potential development on public lands. "NEPA's not a planning process, but a cover-your-ass process, so you can prove you discussed everything. It's supposed to be a decision-making tool in critical aspect, but it's really done after the fact."

We stopped at the edge of meadowland that ran for miles to the northeast. Exxon's man, young and assertive, opened a topographic map and made an X on it with a felt-tip pen. A well pad on the edge of the meadow would be easy to service; the construction crew would have plenty of room to move around. And it would be easy to screen with trees—good VRM.

"Out of sight, out of mind," Bruce said, under his breath. Then, aloud, "Leaving roads is the main detriment to wildlife habitat. A road here would cut across the creek and disturb subirrigation of the meadow." The road we came in on had been built to service a previous well in the woods, he added, and should be used again instead of building another.

But the old well site did not suit Exxon. Too small. So Bruce mentioned the unmentionable—directional drilling. That meant getting up on the mountain somewhere and coming down to this gas field at an angle, underground—a million-dollar proposition.

"I know if I go back and talk directional," said Exxon's man, "they'll hit the ceiling. I guess we'll have to go over this again."

It was a process of push and shove suited to bottom-line boardrooms, not high, well-watered meadows in the shadow of quaky and Engelmann spruce, where sandhill cranes clattered by in gangly outrage, and the elk had left an abundance of spore. The hired specialists, including the wildlife man, had said not a word. The soils man took a spade and dug some soil; the veg man peeled a few leaves. But they kept their opinions to themselves; they were on the Exxon payroll.

We headed into the woods to look for an alternate well sight. The woods were wet and thick with deadfall, lovely for wildlife but not so accessible to human beings encumbered with rolled maps, spades, and clipboards. Soon the group was split up and half lost. I found myself with an Exxon man from Houston. He had been recently transferred and was trying to cope with one of the most radical transplantations in the oil patch. He had rented a place up in Jackson because his wife couldn't abide Big Piney—another commuter—and his new boots were full of water darkened by leaf rot.

We straggled back to the pickups. Bruce was already there, his bright red Game and Fish shirt a flag in the midst of forest greens and khaki. Exxon provided sandwiches; we all strung out to eat along the road bank. The Forest Service wanted a smaller pad than what Exxon's plans called for, maybe a tiered one that would cling to the wooded slope. "I think I'd have trouble getting that through," said the Exxon rep. "They moan and complain when I talk about a shorter pad."

"Well, they'll just have to moan and complain," said Bruce. "This is what we have to work with."

Exxon clung to its notion of a pad in the middle of the meadow. Two reps pushed the aesthetics: transplanted aspen to hide a rig and pad. "You'd only have a pickup going in there every eight hours," said one rep. "Is that worse than a camper?"

"The point is, you want to take the disturbance right into the habitat. Let's don't make any hasty decisions," Bruce added. "Check the alternatives—like directional drilling."

That specter was enough to move Exxon out of the meadow and onto the slope at last. They tentatively agreed to a smaller pad on the old site, a strengthened reserve pit, and access by the existing road—a modest victory for bugs and bunnies.

"Hey, don't take it personally," Bruce told the Exxon man. "Get the pressure level down."

He laughed to himself as we drove off. "These guys have got their marching orders, but they're all right." His eyes behind the sunglasses were not amused, however. "You get pretty callous. If you don't, you lose your sanity."

Some spring day, a cow and calf would pause at the edge of the aspens and then step boldly into a meadow where a concrete slab and a color-coordinated shed might have stood, and a road cut for all time. In retrospect, it hardly mattered. This boom petered out at the end of the twentieth century, during which some three thousand wells had been dug in the county, but it was nothing compared with the nightmare of development ushered in by the administration of George W. Bush. Almost two thousand new wells were sunk by

2006, with seven thousand more permitted over the next decade. Most of the precautions taken by people like Bruce would be swept away in the frenzied abandonment of environmental and community standards; the current troubles of the landscape—and the things living in it—would seem quaint by comparison.

I STOPPED BY the Silver Spur to get ice. The sorry-ass cowboy, friend of Red Adair, was still there, wearing only one hat today. His face lit up at the sight of me; he was ready with more abuse for foolish questions. I put my face close to his and said, "We're talking a two-hundred-and-sixteen-square-mile well field and one point three two billion cubic feet of sour gas for a break-out of methane and cee oh two at the rate of four hundred million cubic feet a day with a hydrogen sulfide stripper a hundred and sixty feet high and weighing sixteen hundred tons. . . ."

He looked at me with real hatred.

"Be a good boy," cautioned the barmaid, pouring him a jigger-full of Calvert's.

I got out of town.

Chapter 5

LONG WATER

HIGH IN THE SAWTOOTH MOUNTAINS OF SOUTH-western Idaho, in a collision of granite and blue sky, I go looking for the headwaters of a river and find water of astonishing clarity, where shadows of native trout lie across mottled stone and the icy touch of snowmelt takes my breath away. It's the infant Middle Fork of the Boise River, born to the two-million-acre Boise National Forest that contains more than one thousand miles of tributaries. This sprawling domain of Douglas fir, ponderosa pine, and alpine meadows is the upward extension of the Idaho batholiths, a geologic formation rich in minerals that produced the commodity most precious to early European settlers—gold.

A rush during the Civil War brought Confederate sympathizers who put the river to work, dissolving the banks with water under pressure, to get at the gold. More than a hundred years later, great piles of stone still sadly litter the streambeds, and ancient iron pipes rust in the woods. In 1990, the state and the country were reminded of the destructive legacy of the gold boom and the fragility of river systems. An old log dam gave way and released as much as two hundred thousand cubic yards of silt along with arsenic, mercury, and other toxins, gold-mining by-products that had been trapped for more than a century.

Above the South Fork of the Boise, blocks of lava and granite lie together in an idyll of plate tectonics. Steep valleys dip from a high, now-arid range and sage flats; the canyon narrows as the river descends past wildflowers—Indian paintbrush, rocket penstemon, blue lupine—gathering speed. But man-made complications affect inky blue reservoirs in canyons downstream, slowly filling them with sediments from more than a century of logging. The river plunges into Arrowrock Reservoir, as do the combined Middle and North forks.

This dam was the world's highest when completed in 1916 and still generates hydroelectric power and stores water for agriculture further downstream, as do other dams built on the Boise by the Bureau of Reclamation. The river is just one of many contended over in the West in an increasingly chaotic squabble over this, the most important, diminishing resource—water. The Boise illustrates as well as any river the difficulties of accommodating past and present and haves and have-nots. Overall, the destructive consequences for all rivers start, as they do here, just short of the headwaters and continue all the way to a cold, distant ocean.

After dispersion through concrete ditches, river water is shot from sprinklers mounted on wheels that creep across vast emerald fields; although officially the property of the residents of surrounding states, the river is really controlled by a relatively few corn, bean, and potato farmers who have transformed its naturally arid shores. In dry years, crops get water at the expense of everything else. The Bureau of Reclamation is told what to do by irrigators whose antecedents laid claim to the entire river on the assertion that they got there first, an argument that annoys the director of Idaho Rivers United. "The *fish* got there first," she points out repeatedly, "but the early irrigators divided the river up among themselves."

The Boise also has an urban life, with skateboarders instead of elk dominating banks once shaded by cottonwood trees. Cut off from its headwaters by towering dams, the river, like most rivers in the West, is used extensively by human beings for power, farming, and recreation. Tubers carrying coolers and kids by the thousands bob through the city of Boise, and on hot summer weekends, the river resembles a kind of aquatic bumper-car concession. There's a river festival, yet this stretch of river can still yield an eight-pound trout.

Fought over by federal and local agencies, it sustains

innumerable other creatures, but rainbows and browns are severely stressed in the winter, when water is impounded for irrigation and levels fall. Other wildlife, including deer, mink, and beaver, suffers, too, and when the water returns to the Boise further downstream, it's laced with fertilizers and pesticides. All this occurs at a time when clean, free-flowing water and what surrounds it have become prestigious assets all over America—and particularly in the state where "Scenic Idaho" outranks "Famous Potatoes" on license plates. Getting there first may be the basis for most Western water law, but increasingly, people in Idaho and elsewhere are asking the questions: Who owns the rivers, and who is ultimately responsible for them?

Boise's administrator of the Parks and Recreation Department and a member of the Ted Trueblood Chapter of Trout Unlimited calls it "a life-line for the city, a place where people come to relax and rejuvenate," the same claim made for rivers by the Romans, who passed laws assuring that no individuals or groups could appropriate this communal boon. Land for paths on both sides of the Boise River was either donated or acquired by easement. Bike paths were so well used that speed limits had to be imposed.

The city of Boise's drinking water comes from wells, as does that of the new communities that have risen jarringly to the south and west of the city, part of Idaho's ongoing real estate boom. The land may no longer be in agricultural production, but the water once available to the old owners isn't available to the new owners, because of the peculiarities of Western water law. Householders aren't farmers, so the water goes into a kind of water bank behind the dams, to be used by irrigators, who pay ridiculously little for it.

They are well served by the Idaho Water Users Association, an organization made up of a hundred irrigators in as many irrigation districts with the power to tax and to elect their directors. "Water rights are property rights," the director says. When I ask about the possibility of giving more water to people and fish, he adds, "Reallocation is equated with socialism."

Thirty years ago, a "minimum flow" was agreed upon by various agencies involved in river management. This agreement recognized that the river should contain at least 150 cubic feet per second, or *cfs*—I have heard a lot about cfs in Idaho—supposedly enough water to offer minimum protection to fish and other wildlife. But even minimum flow is subject to the willingness of irrigators to give up water in dry years. They own all of the Boise when the river is low and so can get as much water as the person in charge is willing to give them. He is the "water master," paid by the irrigators, and, in Idaho, as the director says, "is essentially God."

God's name is Buddy, and he wears a striped golf shirt, jeans, and white sneakers and works in downtown Boise in an old brick building that housed Water District No. 63. On his office wall hangs the mounted head of an elk he shot with a bow and arrow. "My job," he says, "is to dictate the flow of the river, so that it reaches the proper head gates and people get the water to which they are entitled." He was chosen to do this by the water district's board of directors, who "hold a little formal election and set a budget." He was then rubber-stamped by the Idaho Department of Water Resources, which gave him the authority to tell the powerful Bureau of Reclamation how much water to release from the dams, and when.

We get into the red pickup he uses to check out two hundred miles of the Boise. "We call it a working river," he says. By "we," he means the Bureau of Reclamation, the Army Corps of Engineers, the state's nonprofit canal companies and irrigation districts, the city of Boise, and, I suppose, the Idaho Department of Fish and Game. He believes unequivocally in water law: "The recreationists and the fish don't pay anything for the use of irrigators' water."

God wishes to check the water monitoring stations in the middle reaches of the Boise and drives to the Ridenbaugh Canal, one of the largest in the system, and unlocks a corrugated iron hut containing a water gauge that records the depth, width, and velocity of the water in the canal. A "ditch rider" stops by, a local overseer who occupies a place further down the hydrologic totem pole. If the ditch rider needs more water, God calls the Bureau of Reclamation at the Lucky Peak Dam and tells them to release some. Pronto.

The water master's divine status was questioned by the fisheries coordinator of the Idaho Department of Fish and Game. "The irrigators still hold most of the cards," he told me earlier, "but people want to see water in the river. Period."

More and more people around the West are talking about taking water from irrigators and power generators and giving it to communities, wildlife, and recreation-ists. And the man responsible for storing the Boise's water, the local director of the Bureau of Reclamation in Boise, admits that eventually "we'll have reallocation." He winced, knowing such an admission would cause him political problems. "It will come, but not in my lifetime. You're talking revolution."

DOWNSTREAM, the Boise takes on the character of most rivers in America: a roiling, putty-colored medium for chemicals, treated waste, and silt. Near the mouth stands what was left of the river's first European settle-ment, Fort Boise, once the property of the Hudson's Bay Company, before flooding took down the old adobe walls in 1853 and American Indians scared off the survi-vors. The Boise flows leisurely through state land thick with cattails, creek-side willows, quail, and magpies, looking almost tropical, lazily blending with the Snake River, which is larger and also freighted with agricultural runoff and other problems but on a much larger scale.

From there I travel downstream—north—by car, on the Idaho-Oregon border, touching and retouching the Snake. At the town of Nyssa, Oregon, a sugar-beet processing plant smells pervasively of something large and thoroughly dead. Then the Payette River flows in strongly from the east, but the free-flowing Snake soon slackens in a dust-hazed reservoir. Standing water has sucked at the shoreline, leaving signs of erosion, extend-ing fifty-three miles to Brownlee Dam, a huge rock pile with a spillway trailing braids of water into yet another reservoir.

The Snake extends monotonously for a few more miles to Oxbow Dam. Below it, the river flows briefly but soon dies in a long, fjordlike backwater extending to the Hells Canyon Dam, the arid mountains burning bright green in the creases where river birch grow. The 318-foot Hells Canyon dam, built in 1967, chokes off the runs of salmon and steelhead in the Snake, the Boise, and other rivers, when from time immemorial the fish have reached as far as Wyoming and Nevada; the structure also drowns one of the most spectacular canyons in the country.

This concrete stopper emits a thin whine: turbines. Downstream lies the Hells Canyon Recreation Area, where I can see the river picking up speed, its volume tremendous. There are no roads there, and no irrigators in a stretch of river among the most dramatic in the West. The only way to reach it quickly, short of plunging in myself, is from downstream.

With misgivings, I avail myself of a homely, controversial invention known as the jet-boat. Thirty-eight feet long, implanted with three V-eight Ford engines that generate eleven hundred horsepower by sucking up water from beneath and blasting it out the stern, the aluminum craft planes northward out of the port of Lewiston, Idaho, the backwater of yet another dam. There are two dozen of us aboard, all tourists except the pilot and a friend, separated from the elements by clear plastic sheeting.

Jet-boats, remarkably loud, constitute an industry in themselves. They burn a gallon of fuel for every half-mile traveled, in this case a hundred miles past columnar basalt formations like rusty iron pinnacles sandwiched together by tectonic pressures, pink mountain flox blooming in the crevices. About thirty miles upstream, where the Nez Perce once had their winter camp, the road and the houses come to an end and the current picks up, working its way down through big, tumbled mountains.

A bighorn sheep stands high on the ramparts, still as stone. "His batteries have run down," says the tour guide. This section of Hells Canyon was declared wild and scenic in 1975, thus protecting it from overuse and development, although it is still used extensively by cows, neither wild nor scenic. The mountains seem immutable, but aren't. Forest once covered large tracts, before people cut the trees and left stone walls along each bank to buttress the trails.

About halfway to the dam, we pass the mouth of the Salmon River on the east side, the longest free-flowing river in the United States and another national treasure. The pilot announces over the loudspeaker, "This is where it all begins," meaning the big rapids that lie ahead of us on the Snake, but he might as well have said that this is where it all ends for spawning salmon that fail to turn left and deadhead at the Hells Canyon Dam. The fish that swim up the Salmon might climb all the way to the east side of the Sawtooth Range.

There is an unreal quality in ascending rapids by jet propulsion. Here the Snake is deep, powerful, untrammeled, ironically the only stretch below Payette where the river can be itself. The Seven Devils wilderness looms on the Idaho side, the seven-thousand-foot ridges of the Wallowa Range in Oregon. We turn back just short of Water Spout Rapid, and I see a couple of back-packers in a distant meadow, staring at us in utter disbelief. The Nez Perce must have stared that way at the old paddle steamers that pushed partway up Hells Canyon a century before, as the European invaders sought the copper and other products in the hills.

THE INLAND PORTS of Lewiston, Idaho, and Clarkston, Washington, with the permanent stench of the big Potlatch pulp mill on the nearby Clearwater River, are created by Lower Granite Dam, one of four dams between Hells Canyon and the Columbia River. The rest of the Snake isn't a river by comparison to what I have seen but a gargantuan float chamber for barges pushing grain and wood products toward the ocean. Dammed rivers are like depressed people: lethargic, slovenly, confused as to direction and purpose. Being thwarted is not good for any living thing, and rivers are alive, although this one seems doomed to the doldrums for the rest of its unnatural life, lying in great troughs of watered farmland so vast it dwindles into haze and thermals.

The Snake joins the Columbia in typical flat water spanned by railroad bridges, parted by the wakes of powerboats, on the outskirts of industrial Pasco, Washington. The Sacajawea State Park sits at the confluence, named for the Shoshone woman who had proved so valuable to Lewis and Clark on their transcontinental trek. They all passed through this country, although today it would be unrecognizable to them.

Just downstream on the Columbia, on the shore of what is called Lake Wallula, stands an industrial complex painted a disconcerting baby-blue—Boise Cascade's pulp mill, blowing smoke of various hues; I smell it long before I make out the huge aerating tank where big nozzles spew dirty brown water into an artificial sea of froth. A sign near the entrance explains that this was a WHITE PAPER DIVISION. One of the chemical compounds in that whiteness is chlorine dioxin, a significant pollutant of this stretch of the Columbia, as is the radioactive leakage from the ground at the Hanford nuclear site just upstream of Pasco, perhaps the worst Superfund site, where nuclear waste was poured into the ground many years ago.

A guard wearing sunglasses and a black uniform with gold chevrons on the collar won't let me in, but I am allowed to talk by telephone to Boise Cascade's public relations officer. She drives out to hand me a brochure informing me that the plant used eighteen million gallons of water to produce six hundred tons of paper a day and burned the equivalent of 780 gallons of oil to do it—a mere 15 percent of the plant's total daily energy consumption, much of it coming from wood chips. The public affairs officer declines to give me a tour, however.

When I ask about dioxin in the river, she says, "The amount of dioxin we produce each year is equal to no more than two aspirin tablets." The problem is that dioxin—a term used for more than two hundred compounds—is the most toxic chemical ever produced and "bioaccumulates" in fish at a rapid rate. Amounts so small they can't be measured cause complications, including cancer, in living organisms.

Thankful to get upwind of the pulp factory, I try to

imagine what a sturgeon on this stretch of river would look like after fifty years of snuffling along the bottom.

LAKE WALLULA is the slack water behind McNary Dam on the Washington-Oregon border, the first below the Snake confluence and the first of four remaining big dams between the Pacific Ocean and me. McNary was completed in 1953, rising 180 feet from the riverbed. I go inside to view the fourteen massive generators that produce 8.6 million megawatt-hours of electricity a year; they are lined up in a room a quarter of a mile long. Workers in hard hats ride tricycles across the vast, spotless tile floor, a surreal sight; I can feel vibrations of the river raging through its artificial sinkholes below each generator, but can't imagine what a four-inch salmon smolt might feel, subjected to the roar of the turbines and often to their blades, what amounts to fourteen Brobdingnagian Cuisinarts.

Collectively, the turbines on the Columbia and Snake destroy 90 percent of the young salmon trying to get downriver. A diversion system has been set up similar to that at other dams, whereby some smolts are directed by screens into a sluice-pipe. From there the fish are transported downriver, with variable rates of mortality. McNary's system resembles a waterslide for fish, plastic spaghetti on stilts, part of a stressful process during which the smolts are screened, shot into high-velocity channels, crowded together, sorted, handled, and pumped into barges or tank trucks.

I see a truck on the road, property of the U.S. Army Corps of Engineers. The driver has stopped for a Coke on his ten-hour drive from Lower Granite Dam, where he picked up five thousand juvenile salmon and steelhead for their three-hundred-mile trip to the tailrace of the Bonneville Dam. The truck contains thirty-five hundred gallons of the Snake River that is being short-circuited, like the fish, to the Columbia. It's cooled by a refrigeration unit and shot through with oxygen from metal tanks. The driver and I climb up and he grips a hatch handle. "If the fish are healthy," he says, "they'll dive as soon as they see the light." The mass of three-inch fingerlings does indeed flee to the shadows.

Perhaps twenty million salmon and steelhead once swam upstream. Now less than one-tenth that number return each year. The mortality rate of the returning salmon is also high, but nothing like the obliteration of the smolts swimming toward the sea. Everyone recognizes the cause of the problem, the impoundment of water behind concrete walls that raises the temperature of the river, spoils spawning beds, prolongs migration, confuses fish, and contributes to their physical destruction. But few people in positions of influence are willing to call for any human sacrifice at all to save the salmon.

The Snake River sockeye salmon have become endangered, and some chinook salmon have climbed onto the threatened-species list. The beneficiaries of dead salmon in the Pacific Northwest are the people who receive cheap electricity because of the dams put in at federal expense by the Army Corps of Engineers. Industry is even more blessed—or damned—particularly the aluminum processors that receive what amounts to subsidized power and the support of politicians. But salmon are a riverine version of the spotted owl, with more potential for economic disruption, and for this reason, the various agencies involved have been reluctant to face the inevitable.

In 1994, the various agencies had been jolted by a Portland federal judge who rejected the plan put forward by the Commerce Department's National Marine Fisheries Service for salmon management. The plan, the judge said, was "too heavily geared to the status quo." Marine Fisheries, the Army Corps of Engineers, the Bureau of Reclamation, and the Bonneville Power Administration had taken, he ruled, "relatively small steps, minor improvements and adjustments when the situation literally cries out for a major overhaul." The struggle goes on today, the fish in worse shape than ever and with more judicial rulings that point toward a showdown in the near future.

At the confluence of the Umatilla and Columbia rivers, I go to talk to the chairman of the board of trustees of the Confederated Tribes of the Umatilla Reservation. The American Indians of the Columbia River basin historically depended upon the salmon and are today in an unpleasant bind, trying to pursue tradition with a dwindling resource. "We have been fishing for salmon forever," he says. "We are part of their lives, and they of ours. Salmon are honored in our religion; we feel a responsibility to them."

He wears his hair in two black braids, but is otherwise indistinguishable from any other American in a golf shirt and chinos. He compares the ceremonial catching of a first salmon by a young American Indian to a bar mitzvah. His great-great-grandfather, a Walla Walla chief, was massacred by Oregon regulars from The Dalles in 1855; the chairman speaks of this as if it had happened last year. He's most eloquent on the subject of rivers, "the earth's lifeblood."

The confederated tribes have long been criticized for continuing to take fish in a time of dwindling numbers, but he points out that the numbers involved in their netting are relatively small. Even those cynical about American Indians netting fish can't argue with the Indian prescription for ailing salmon and steelhead runs: release more water, and stop the increasing dependence upon artificial means of propagation through trucking, barging, and the construction of more and more hatcheries.

I DRIVE WEST, along the Columbia, Mount Hood hanging in the distance and the Columbia River Gorge all around me. The natural defiles and hanging waterfalls seem incomparably grand, the river a mighty moving sea. I try to forget what I now know is just below the surface for the palpable pleasure the visuals provide; ahead lies Portland, where the Willamette River enters, but for the moment, I'm done with this thread of a long, gorgeous, complicated story.

Chapter 6

WEST SLOPE

He ran a string of twenty-four horses in the East Creek drainage of the San Juan Mountains, trailing hunters up through ponderosa and quaking aspen to base camps where a cook fed them hot biscuits and grilled steaks, and then he set them on elk and deer stands in the clear, frosty beauty of the southwest Colorado dawn. He was an outfitter, with one of the best client-kill ratios in the state for bull elk and corporate customers he had developed after watching a Louisiana oilman write out a single check for a party of hunters in his employ. They paid $2,500 apiece for at least the proximity of big game and scenery as far from sales meetings and computers as they could get.

The outfitter didn't ride a horse on those excursions or when he took summer dudes up toward the Weminuche Wilderness; he rode a mule. He had bought it cheap from people who couldn't handle it. A mule's gait was smoother than a horse's, and the narrower girth made a mule a more comfortable mount. The outfitter had a slipped disc, and riding was a bit of a problem. So was walking. He had broken his left ankle so often that his boots had to be high and tight fitting, like a hiker's. His left shoulder socket had the disconcerting habit of separating from the ball. Some of his teeth were broken, and the gaps showed when he smiled. His eyes reacted painfully to too much sunlight, which shone in abundance in the San Juans. He was somewhat deaf, yet could hear an elk breaking timber at quite a distance. On those occasions, he would shake his head and then lean back and rub his lower back in the speculative manner of a mountain man at home with old injuries.

Dan was twenty-nine years old. We met him on the shore of Vallecitos Reservoir after telephoning ahead for reservations, as is required of dudes—me, Penny, and our two daughters, Jessica and Susanna, all of us fresh from a raft descent of the San Juan River in Utah. But this was to be different: Not only would someone cook for us, but shade was also included in the price, and a means of conveyance that, unlike a raft, would stop on command and let the passenger off. And we might discover that some vestiges of the proverbial mountain man had been preserved on the federal domain, meaning U.S. Forest Service land.

Jess, an accomplished equestrian, had a droll view of riding in a saddle with a horn, having learned the sport on a leather postage stamp in Virginia and Maryland. Since Susanna loved all animals, the idea of sitting on one for hours engendered euphoria. Penny's view of horses could best be described as skeptical. None of us expected to be led by a young man in camouflage fatigues and who looked more like a Green Beret than a cowboy.

Dan took us up a dirt road into the San Juan National Forest, where a dozen horses and a mule were tied to a rope strung between two trees, the most rudimentary base camp. His stories began almost immediately, a curious blend of wilderness prowess and violence that didn't seem to have changed much since the days of Jedediah Smith and Kit Carson. One story ran into another with admirable, seamless transition. I couldn't tell which were true, if any, but all were delivered with an earnestness that held us like flypaper.

He and his brothers had gone to school south of Durango, Colorado, at a time when so-called Chicano separatism made things uncomfortable for Anglos. Dan was a star football player—the source of a couple of injuries—who kept a Beasley Colt in his locker. He had learned the quick draw and hip shooting from his father and had drilled holes, he said, in many a plate thrown into the air at exhibitions of Old West prowess. It was a family tradition, his great-grandfather having been run out of Oklahoma for gun fighting. As an old man on a cane, he had asked to heft Dan's pistol, and then fired and hit a Coke can tossed into the air. "They don't balance 'em the way they used to," the old man said.

The pistol and Dan's reputation for quick draw made any bad boys reluctant to jump him. He then told another story of a harrowing battle in the desert, when half a dozen of his friends and relatives stood off forty enemies with their fists, an encounter that Dan claimed made the Denver papers and brought in the FBI. That story ended with cars being pushed over a cliff—and Susanna rolling her eyes in disbelief. Dan's tales belonged to a tradition of hyperbole that went back to campfire yarns and dime novels about Deadwood Dick and other wild men of the fictional West. "There you will see action," Walter Prescott Webb wrote in *The Great Plains,* "experience adventure, hear strange new words, and see a relationship between man and man, man and horses, man and cattle, man and woman, that you will find nowhere else in America."

Henry Nash Smith pointed out that writers about the West "had to struggle against the notion that their characters had no claim upon the attention of sophisticated readers, except through their alarming or at best their picturesque lack of refinement."

We set out the following morning with Dan's wife and their daughter, nine years old and in thorough control of her bay pony. Her father was to meet us in the high country, after baiting his black bear sites with shortbread and molasses, to draw them in to be filmed for a tourist promo financed by the state. We took our time getting there. Gambel oak and pine turned to Douglas

fir, bigger ponderosa, and quaking aspen. The Weminuche Wilderness sprawled above us, obscured off and
on by clouds that doused us and then let in the light.
Trail rides are excuses to turn off the mind and open the
shutter; the scenes would come back in three-by-four
semiglossies of dandelion-strewn meadows, chipmunks
on lichen-covered boulders, a remote beaver pond clear
as ether draining into a rushing stream where we could
fish as much as we wanted, Dan had said. That was
quite true, although the chance of catching anything in
small rushing streams bordered on nonexistent.

Lolling in nature was the point, the Easterner's common experience in the West. The fondest scenes never
made it onto film: Susanna and me washing off Utah
dirt in that same snowy torrent that would eventually
find its way into the Colorado River; Jess professionally
appraising her horse, a hand on its rump; Penny supine
in dandelions, her hair red-gold in the sun.

Dan rode up in the late afternoon, and his wife went
back to town. He had put on a round hat with a leather
patch sewed over the crown, cinched beneath his chin,
and a patched vest more in keeping with the leather-
stocking's image. We entered dense quakies with blazes
put there by elk that came down hungry at the end of
winter and munched on luminous aspen skin until they
could get at the green shoots beneath the snow.

He had been using this part of the San Juans since
he was twelve. His father had run cattle on the forest and kept a cabin up the drainage, another ranching family without a ranch, and an unhappy history of
failed real estate deals and broken promises. Sometimes

they took hunters in for a fee, courtesy of Uncle Sugar, as he called the federal government. They all slept in the cabin also occupied by a pack rat. One night—Dan said—a client woke up to see it running across a rafter and emptied a nine-shot Luger trying to kill it, bringing every other head up hard against the bunk above, but missing the rat.

We unpacked, setting gear against the smooth bark of the trees and relieving the mounts of their bridles. Dan had found seven watches, he said, in the pack rat's first nest. The rat made another and apparently filled it with sticks of ditching powder, akin to dynamite but more volatile, used by his father to blast out water holes along the creek. Years later, after Dan was married, they came up to spend a weekend at the cabin. Dan saw the rat scramble, drew his pistol, and fanned a couple of .22 Magnum slugs into the hole after it.

His wife, sitting under a tree a quarter of a mile away, thought she heard a sonic boom. She looked up from her book at a mushroom of smoke and wood splinters. When she got down to where the cabin had been, she found her husband lying under a refrigerator, blood flowing from nose and ears. He came awake blind, aware of strange vibrations that were his wife's screams. "I thought the gun blew up," he said. "But then I thought, 'Too big for that.' I felt like I was on fire. She tied a bandana around my eyes, which is the only reason I can see today. It kept the light of the sun off my skinned eyeballs."

His horse had refused to let him on, because of all the blood. "She got me onto her horse and led me down the mountain. Every time I'd start to go into shock, another tree branch would whap me on the head and wake me up. That saved my life." The doctors wanted him in the hospital for three months, but he got up, he said, after ten days and went home. "My wife took care of me. My eyes were blobs of green ooze"—even Susanna was listening now—"but I didn't have hardly a scratch on me, just a hole in my big toe where the blast had driven a nail through."

Dan was a good outfitter by most accounts, including his own. He washed his hair every morning in the woods, to banish human smells, and dusted with baking powder for the same reason. He packed his clothes in pine needles. On scouting trips, he took a sack of potatoes and ate them raw, like apples, and beef he had jerked in a tepee he built next to his trailer outside Durango. He made salads of dandelion greens. He roasted cattails like popcorn and peeled and sliced the inner shoots—"Delicious"—and made willow bark tea for headaches, a kind of Rocky Mountain natural aspirin.

"Total granola," said Jess, heaving her saddle over an aspen bough.

I was worried about dinner now. Dan built a fire in a ring of blackened rocks and, from the canvas-covered wooden larder, produced not seeds and shoots and scraps of bark but thick pork chops, potatoes, milk, lettuce, salad dressing, hot chocolate, instant coffee, Miracle Whip, and cookies. After supper, Dan's daughter sang sweetly in a high, tremulous voice, with a trace of country twang and considerable polish. In the firelight, she looked older and wiser than the rest of us, and decidedly urban, roughing it because her daddy was. The sight would have made me miserable if my own children hadn't been there beside her. I wondered if Susanna was a bit jealous of her theatrical polish and the fact that she knew the words of a whole country-western number, but if so, she didn't show it.

All three girls crawled into the bottomless pup tent Dan had pitched, and they unrolled their sleeping bags. "Gross," said Jess, the object of opprobrium being the saddle mats. They smelled of horse and mule, having gone directly onto the ground from those sweaty backs. "Lucky girls," said Dan. "Them mats make the softest bed in the woods."

The situation was not Total Granola, but it wasn't Best Western, either. Jess may have been fond of horses, but sleeping on a strange one's underwear didn't appeal to her, and one of the mats had come off a mule. In the end, they all lay down on them.

There was no moon. A paradoxically black, luminous sky arched over the San Juans, seen through the lattice-work of aspen boughs still as death. Dan split pieces of quaky logs and fed them into the walled fire; I mixed another cup of hot chocolate, grateful for the heat in my hands. Penny crawled into the cold bedroll. We had never had a tent pitched for us; it seemed the height of luxury, but you paid for it.

The horses stomped their feet, used to this rustic corral. Dan kept it in some semblance of order, in the unlikelihood that a Forest Service ranger would pass through. Dan paid little more than a thousand dollars a year for the use of the forest, including about two hundred acres he considered his own. He was allowed four hundred and fifty visitor days—the measure of use of public lands—but the arrangement was fairly fluid; if he got a good response from his mailing, he called the secretary in Bayfield and worked out an extension. The district ranger apparently knew little about outfitters and cared less; he had hard lumber targets to worry about and roads to build.

Hunters were his bread and butter. They paid to go into the wilderness for eleven days, but usually stayed no more than five before a sufficient number of elk had been killed, a very profitable arrangement even when he factored in the steaks, the cook, and the extra guide. Not all the clients had to get an elk; many just wanted to get drunk. Sometimes the men and not the animals died. Two years before, a client had a massive heart attack on a stand. Dan said, "I ran the elk right past him, but he messed up and didn't shoot. He tried to follow them over the ridge. Nine times out of ten, an inexperienced hunter will try to chase elk. He wasn't on the stand when I went to pick him up. I got back to camp, and he wasn't there, either. The others told me he had already had one heart attack, and I knew right then that he was dead.

"I went back and found him right on the trail, where he had fallen. He must have died instantly because he hadn't tore up the ground, or anything. Rigor mortis had set in. I had a hell of a time getting him on that horse. If you get a man right after he's died, you can get him over the saddle, but he was straight and stiff, and a big man. I got him up to the top of the ridge, covered him with some horse blankets and the saddle, and went back for him the next morning. We built a travois to haul him out, and that worked for a while. Then something spooked the horse. I never knew a horse could run with a travois. I thought, 'His family's gonna hate me for tearing him up,' but when we turned the body over, there wasn't a mark on it."

The trunks of the aspens looked ghostly in the firelight. Dan added, "This is my little kingdom." Other outfitters might pass through but rarely did, and never camped in the grove. The territorial imperative among outfitters in the West was loose but real, and without legal foundation. Their hoof-carved ruts laced the national forests, and pack strings were the hallmark of high stands of ponderosa and Engelmann spruce. They shared the trail with backpackers, an uneasy accommodation—the same old animosity between cowboy and sodbuster mirrored in outfitters and hikers. The view from a saddle was better, granted, but it affected people in strange ways, bringing out fatal arrogance in some.

I could see how it was easier to shoot someone from a saddle than with your feet planted on the ground. The national forests were full of overweight men with guns strapped to their legs for protection against grizzlies that had once lived in these big, wrinkled mountains, but these men would now need an airline ticket to reach the bears. With Winchesters shoved into rifle slings, the outfitters loaded their pack horses with collapsible boats, electric motors, cases of beer, acres of plastic sheeting to protect themselves and their clients from the outdoors, and an occasional cast-iron stove for baking biscuits and preparing Irish coffee. Much of that junk they left in the woods for unfortunate Forest Service volunteers to haul out, when the service should have hired a gunslinger to go after them for the slovenly outlaws they were.

An outfitter who rode a mule and wore hiking boots set a fine example, in my estimation, even if those accoutrements derived from chronic accidents in his short, violent life. That he considered this area his kingdom proved that the notion of the West hadn't changed in some ways in two centuries, except that those kingdoms were now the relative size of postage stamps.

The history of public lands from that time is both hideously complicated and quite simple. They derive from conquest, purchase, and the plain fact of occupancy, forever different because of their acquisition after nationhood. Six of the original colonies had clearly prescribed boundaries based upon grants from Great Britain; the other seven included territories ambling off in the general direction of the Mississippi, of vague metes and bounds, and few tenants who were not aboriginal. After independence, those seven states ceded their surplus territory to the new federal government under the Articles of Confederation as an equalizing measure and a means of raising revenue. This was the "public domain," frontier lands given in payment for military service and others sold in speculation, and states carved out of them entered the Union on an equal basis.

"Westward the star of Empire takes its course," said John Quincy Adams at Plymouth Rock in 1802. No matter that he meant western Pennsylvania or maybe Ohio; that way lay the future. The Louisiana Purchase, the Oregon Compromise, and a victorious war with

Mexico added new possibility for what became an unprecedented boon to the landless willing to take a risk, and a significant national character trait. Americans were bound to move west, by right and destiny, or so the argument went. A magazine editor named John L. Sullivan excoriated foreign countries in 1845 for "limiting our greatness and checking the fulfillment of our manifest destiny to overspread the continent allotted by Providence for the free development of our yearly multiplying millions."

Those multiplying millions were at first reluctant to die at the hands of "savages" or to starve in country rough beyond their imagining; they had to be oratorically prodded out of eastern cities. By the time of the Civil War, most land not too rough or dry to be plowed had come into private ownership, much of it through fraud. The roughest and driest lay west of the Rockies. The Homestead Acts and a string of uncommonly wet years moved nesters into places unfit for farming or other human sustenance. Boosters like William Gilpin proclaimed that moisture followed the plow and that firewood lay under the sand and that, in short, agrarian culture could modify this climate and landscape.

Droughty years moved many of the nesters off again, their land going into cattle spreads that had already damaged the range. Private holdings clung to river and stream banks, natural springs, low meadow, and farmland that could be irrigated; what was left—the proverbial lands nobody wanted—lacked water or offered too much resistance to settlement. Mountainous, wooded terrain eventually went into the Forestry Bureau, and the arid stuff into the Grazing Service, which became the Bureau of Land Management. The government still owned about a third of the land mass consisting of New Mexico, Arizona, California, Nevada, Utah, Oregon, Washington, Idaho, Montana, Wyoming, and Colorado—unwitting vessels of a national treasure that came into being almost by inadvertence.

By 1890, cattle and sheep dominated the West. That year, the Bureau of the Census announced for the first time that it had been unable to discover a frontier between wild and settled areas. But the West as a state of mind was incalculably important to Americans, whether or not one had the intention of going there. "American social development has been continually beginning over again on the frontier," Frederick Jackson Turner wrote in 1893, in his famous celebration of Manifest Destiny. "This perennial rebirth, this fluidity of American life, this expansion westward with its new opportunities . . . furnish the forces dominating American character."

Some of that character still exists in the West, thanks to public lands, which have harbored certain quirky, unruly, even dangerous states of mind, many directed against the system that offers refuge. Landscape has something to do with it, its basic discomfort, aridity, and intransigence, as well as its beauty. Western institutions— the cowboy and the mountain man—would not have endured even in Dan's form without access to public lands, free for all practical purposes, free in fact for most. The land serves as a reservoir for values that originally brought people onto the public domain— a desire for improvement, material and imaginative, and escape.

But that frontier has gone from natural to bureaucratic, deprived of such vital competitors as railroad magnates, buffalo slayers, American Indians, and grizzlies, but rich with their contemporary equivalents. Today the frontier is a stomping ground for lawyers—corporate and environmental—developers, and political appointees to federal agencies that are supposed to protect the public lands but instead arrange for their resources to be given away to friends and supporters.

I crawled into bed. Dan slept outside in his canvas roll without benefit of a tent. The next morning, he would be up before dawn, washing his hair in the runoff from the Weminuche.

II. BACK EAST

Chapter 7

NEW ORLEANS

The hurricane and I arrived in New Orleans only two days apart. I happened to get there first and spent a day ignoring laconic suggestions that a hurricane was more important than renting an apartment. Impending weather is of little concern to the young; the night it struck, I sat with a friend who lived above a garage in the Garden District, drinking Dixie beer and listening to the palms' death rattle. We went out for a walk at midnight—what a trip!—our hats disappearing and the rain stinging our faces. We heard for the first time the keening of wind at high velocity and saw power lines dancing as if possessed and trees shedding their leaves like evening gloves. The air, laden with flotsam moving too fast to be identified, bore the weight of moisture suddenly malevolent, gathering strength and weapons for a brawl. It was a brawl we could not escape except by crawling back up the steps and leaning the door shut against projectile rain but not, of course, silencing the amazing racket such a storm entails.

It was Betsy, not Katrina, and during that night in September 1965, it rode a ten-foot storm surge into the city and did more than a billion dollars' worth of damage, the first such hurricane to achieve that dubious distinction. We emerged the next morning to find prostrate live oaks on all sides; overhead, the gunmetal sky lacked depth but not foreboding. All around lay a silence that plainly said that something terrible had occurred and that to go forth was to risk encountering a new reality. But we had things to do—he worked in a bank and I was to begin reporting for the daily *Times-Picayune*—and so we put on our suits and ventured forth in his old Chevy, rolling over a carpet of broken boards, glass, and vegetation.

St. Charles Avenue looked like a lumber camp waiting for the saw; big trees stretched across streetcar tracks like gigantic railroad ties. We weaved back and forth over the rails to avoid them, the only moving thing in sight, a pea-green voyager with tail fins adrift in a calamitous dreamscape. Gorgeous antebellum homes provided a somber backdrop, their lawns trashed and magnolias deflowered and facades punctuated by the black holes of smashed windows, but still luminous, proud in misfortune, broad porch roofs held up by Corinthian columns and carved acanthus leaves untroubled on their pediments.

The first people we saw were men who lived in the missions and cheap hotels around Lafayette Square, gathered outside the Cave Inn, a notorious dive, as if it might open on this of all days and provide some alcoholic relief for a colossal morning after. I got out of the car and walked into the darkened building that housed the newspaper and the presses, up four flights of stairs to editorial, and across a deserted wood floor branded with a thousand cigarette butts. It was early; no one else had as yet managed the commute. In the light from the big windows, I sat and read back issues until, two hours later, a silhouette appeared at the far side of the cavernous room. The city editor, carrying a suit jacket over his shoulder, stopped, and I told him I was the new reporter. He gazed out at curtains trailing from broken windows and said wearily, "Go and write a story about the effects of the storm on the city."

I was an English major and had never written a news story; I knew next to nothing about New Orleans. So I wandered from Poydras Street down to the French Quarter, ate a bowl of turtle soup in the only restaurant I found open, and interviewed a dozen people whose houses had lost shingles and whose basements had water in them. I did not even suspect that a mile to the east were the real, low-lying disaster areas, the city's poorest and most violent.

The Quarter had weathered the storm better than most neighborhoods, having been built on the driest ground with much thought given to the power of the Mississippi River, an example of Old World restraint in sharp contrast to the sheer opportunism of today. The original French and Spanish settlers—Creoles—had been added to by Anglos, relative latecomers, and this, the original city, was by the middle of the nineteenth century viewed somewhat disapprovingly by the new ruling elite who had moved into those houses on St. Charles, on the upriver, "American" side of Canal Street.

I went back to the office dazed not by the interviews but by the sensory power of this remarkable place and wrote a feeble story, only to see it appear on page one of the first edition because no other reporter had showed up to write a better one. I thought I had seen what a storm could do, but I was wrong. Over the next two weeks, I worked fourteen hours a day in parts of the city not as lucky as the Quarter and experienced for the first time in my life what most of humanity faces regularly: violence, deprivation, hunger, unalterable sadness.

In the chaos of the municipal auditorium converted to a refugee shelter, a distraught man pleaded with me to help him find a daughter lost in the six feet of water standing in the streets of the Ninth Ward. Mothers with stunned children in tow inquired about drinking water, patient in their desperation. The city provided some assistance, but neither it nor the state—nor the feds—had prepared for this. People moved as if in slow motion, confused and ultimately bored with so much loss, but there was more resignation than crime, more accommodation of loss than denunciation of authority.

By then I had found an apartment on Prytania Street, in an antebellum shotgun house with wide cypress floorboards, a balcony, water-streaked walls, and furniture I began assembling from the Salvation Army, anticipating the arrival of Penny and Brennan, then an infant. The comparison between my harried but relatively easy existence and that of the people I wrote about was inescapable. Some eighty of them had died in Betsy, whose damage to Louisiana covered five thousand square miles and displaced a quarter of a million citizens, a stunning figure in those days.

The flooding had exposed the weakness of the levees, the inadequacy of the massive pumps moving water ceaselessly from this shallow dish of a city. Soon after the storm, public vows were made to fix these problems. Meanwhile, it was back to business: The bars opened, followed by the restaurants, then those places with less interesting transactions.

From this reassertion of the diurnal sprang the natural stimulants that had made the city famous and indelibly scored the imaginations of American writers from Lafcadio Hearn to Walker Percy. There is no adequate preparation for the garlic-laden air blown from restaurant exhaust fans, the aroma of Colombian coffee roasting in the Irish Channel, the gentle decline of oyster shells dumped on roads, and the silty presence of a mighty river unseen beyond the levee but never forgotten; the tastes of roux, andouille sausage, crabs in every imaginable pose, red beans and rice, cold beer and hot brewed chicory, and warmed-over roast beef and gravy slathered on French bread assaulted with a butcher knife and shoved under your nose as if a basic right of all humanity. There was Dixieland, of course, and jazz funerals, but also the music of a new generation of artists below Esplanade Avenue; also Creole cadences and bits of Cajun in from the west country, local black intoning, and the greeting of poor white boys also living below sea level. *Wheah ya't, ya mothuh?*

In the two years that followed, I came to know the city well, in large part because I volunteered for the police beat and every morning rode the bus and walked through the tough Claiborne Street neighborhood to the combined courthouse, police station, and parish prison on Tulane Avenue. There I undertook the recording of transgressions that defied the imagination, starting with the snatching of heads from a crypt in the cemetery across the street from Commander's Palace . . . but enough of that. I learned that my chosen city was corrupt, racist, dangerous—an assaulter of livers with pousse-cafés and every other known drink consumed as matter of course; a clogger of arteries with deep-fried oysters, crawfish étouffée, and gumbo ya-ya; a menacer of mind with too much heat and ease; the occasional outright destroyer by storms and a citizen packing steel or a cop in a bad mood—but also quite wonderful.

Inherent in the city's overwhelming presence was a palpable past. You heard it in footsteps on old wooden stairs in the Pontalba apartments that flank Jackson Square, in tugboat whistles and the hawking of produce in the Decatur Street market; you saw it in the moldering depths of the Cabildo and the pews of St. Louis Cathedral, where parishioners outnumbered tourists and

Mass arose as it had for two hundred years, in fourteen-foot ceilings and the superstructure of ships rising above the warehouses along Magazine Street. Listen to the clatter of the trolley, and smell the acrid electric flash as the streetcar turns into St. Charles from Canal; feel the cobblestones through your soles; touch wrought-iron balconies installed on street-flush Gallic houses; stare at ornate plaster, pagan faces carved into fountains hidden away behind old brick walls, and cascading bougainvillea sighing in the night breeze.

Life had not yet been squeezed out of history as it has in many places; the past could not be laminated, because it was still being lived, it was real. So were all the problems of humanity. I eventually wrote a novel about all this and called it *The Big Easy,* a name I had never seen in print and whose explanation I overheard in a conversation between two black men eating po'boys. The phrase meant, one man explained, that with all the amenities and love of existence in New Orleans, if you couldn't make it here, you couldn't make it anywhere.

Watching the awful aftermath of hurricane Katrina on television in September 2005, I realized that forty years had passed since Betsy and that although the effects of the earlier hurricane had been a mere cameo of this one, all the weaknesses of the system had been revealed then. Despite the promises to fix them, little notice had really been taken. The decision to build a massive hurricane barrier had been officially ordained, and congressional approval granted, but it was never built. Consequently, much that informed the notion of historic and spiritual New Orleans was gone forever.

New Orleans is by temperament a Mediterranean city, infused with both fatalism and a tolerance that once seemed equal even to hurricanes. Though it may be again, something basic seems to have changed: the perception of the city, and of the country of which New Orleans is such a valuable piece, by everyone. Its problems, like America's, were as old as the republic. How ironic that this exotic, accepting place had revealed, against its wishes and to its great hardship, so much that is wrong. Not only were the city's—and by implication, the country's—poor floated up by this hurricane for the world to see, but so was the basic inadequacy, and worse, of our rulers, elected and otherwise. Bobbing in the Big Uneasy's flooded streets, along with corpses and the ugly detritus of our consumer society, were racial discrimination, official ineptitude, congressional perfidy, and, at the apex of American politics, incompetence bordering on the criminal.

Insight may be the ultimate service provided to us all by a city older, more interesting, and more enduring than most. Yet many former residents of New Orleans never returned to what was once home. Inherent in this particular tragedy is the fact that natural lessons unheeded in a complicated, increasingly fragile world dominated by politics and short-term economic advantage entail human misery and cultural annihilation no society can survive for long.

Chapter 8

DRY TORTUGAS

On the far side of the Gulf of Mexico from New Orleans, exposed to a great variety of natural threats and deprived of fresh water altogether, is a spit of sand that also attracts a disproportionate number of human visitors, as well as nesting hawksbill, loggerhead, and green turtles, and whole populations of sooty and noddy terns. Because it provides a layover for many species of birds migrating between the United States and Africa and South America, I and fifty members of the Tropical Audubon Society stand at the rail of the 105-foot *Yankee Freedom* experiencing a collective hallucination: sunlit sea the color of cobalt and limes, hexagonal brick ramparts half a mile in circumference, half a dozen bastions like monumental spear points above a reflecting moat, gunports, and, through the archway, buttonwood and gumbo-limbo trees.

The parapets of Fort Jefferson, in the Dry Tortugas, are manned not by soldiers but by a handful of figures in Bermudas or thongs, gazing down at a little, powdery beach and wondering why they have come to an obsolete pile of bricks seventy miles west of Key West. Supposedly the largest masonry structure in the Western Hemisphere, the fort is associated with slavery, the Civil War, presidential assassination, pestilence, shipwreck, and imprisonment. But it speaks to the contemporary imagination quite differently: a romantic evocation of unspoiled reefs and unblemished maritime landscapes that is illusory and threatened by a phenomenon— tourism—today more powerful and persistent than a hurricane.

WITHIN THE HOUR, I'm sitting in a 21-foot Boston Whaler with a U.S. National Park Service ranger, listening to a conversation about Porta-Potties. Not their efficiency, but their drawbacks. His plastic web belt supports handcuffs, a steel club, and a .40-caliber automatic pistol. An ample young woman in a swimsuit sits on the edge of a sailing catamaran, *Mister Toad's Wild Ride,* and leans over him. She is one of some eighty thousand visitors a year and has just been told that she can't dump her seven-gallon portable john into the harbor. "Well," she says, "we can dump it at the dock restroom."

"No, you can't. It's already overloaded." The park's septic system has to be pumped out at least three times a year, at $8,000 a pop. A barge has to be dispatched from Key West to carry the sewage away, just one of many large logistical problems. "You've got to go outside park boundaries."

Basically, that means sailing to infinity to flush the toilet. The woman is advised to wait, however, since a black cloud line has been drawn across the northern horizon by a cosmic grease pencil. The Dry Tortugas are known for intense storms that have littered the bottom of the national park's forty square miles with more than two hundred shipwrecks and driven waves into the moat around the fort.

A thousand square miles of ocean contains only one enforcer of the law and an unreckonable number of boaters, tourists, drug runners, poachers, treasure thieves, and convicted criminals. "Lots of felony warrants out there," he says. When he apprehends someone, he has to wait for the Coast Guard to come out and take the culprit away. Many of the arrests involve illegal fishing. The temptations are lobsters twice the size of those found elsewhere in the Florida Straits, and abundant fish. "Poaching is mostly done by sniping at park boundaries," but the radar and the Global Positioning System are down and tonight's patrols have been suspended. And there is the shrimper problem. "When they decide to take a day off and come to the park, it's a disaster. They get drunk and fight. Sometimes there's a woman onboard, and then you get various soap opera scenarios. It's a little lonely," he adds, "boarding a shrimp boat by yourself when they're brawling."

He has keen blue eyes behind rose-tinted sunglasses and a beard that gives him a slightly piratical air, despite his institutional green shorts. The combination bullet-proof vest and life jacket was designed for action; a billed cap covers a head shaved to lapidary smoothness, and in his pocket, he carries a notebook for recording the names of the watercraft in the harbor. "It can save hours of search time if a lost vessel can be put here on a particular day."

A group of men approaches in a dingy from their motor cruiser, not with a Porta-Potty problem but with a fishing one. The ranger explains that they all need licenses, that they might legally keep two fish per day for a total of five, and that the fish have to remain whole until consumed, so that he can count them if he wants to. "No lobstering," he adds, "and no spearfishing."

"No problem," says the skipper. "We're headed for Yucatán."

We are headed for Loggerhead Key, about five miles distant, but the dark line on the northern horizon has gotten thicker. "It's only water," the ranger says, of the rain that is surely coming. A few minutes later, he cuts the engine. A mass of oddly shaped gray clouds is moving ahead of the storm, toward us, perform-ing high arabesques while the wind worries a badly bruised ocean. "I think we're going to get a genuine Tortugas squall."

It is spitting by the time he drops me at the dock. A gale lifts a cloud of dust from the campground, then the towels of sunbathers, who race for the covered dock in a riot of flapping mattresses and overturned coolers. A tent levitates and rolls, snared by the branches of sea grape, while in the harbor boats rear, hauling on their anchor lines. The rain hits in force as I sprint across the drawbridge of the moat, the downpour drowning out the cries of the day-trippers, the wind driving leaves and dirt that sting like shrapnel. A clutch of visitors stands with their faces to the wall, prisoners of a meteorological bombardment.

I take a spiral stone staircase to the second level and make my way along an open corridor, under the long succession of gorgeous brick archways beaten by rain blowing in horizontally through the open gun ports. Beyond the floodwall, waves leap and fling their spray, backed by a wildly fractured sea; the fort seems defenseless, a monolithic impertinence in the midst of tempestuous nature. As the wind slackens, warblers, cuckoos, and indigo buntings flit among the gumbo-limbo trees in the courtyard, stalked by the intrepid birders, their slickers bright yellow and blue in the rain. On the other side of the fort, still in the Boston Whaler, the ranger is untangling lines of boats anchored there and preventing others from being carried off, a lonely, resolute figure no doubt thinking, *It's only water.*

THE OFFICE OF the superintendent of Dry Tortugas National Park has a vaulted brick ceiling that leaks sand and sometimes water onto a valiant air conditioner, a photocopier, and a telephone. The fort cost $3 million to build more than two centuries ago, and today, moisture percolates down into this office and the living quarters of the Park Service personnel. In passageways, little stalagmites of masonry dust rise up from beneath weeping arches; outside, bits of the fort's brick facade fall into the moat. Restoring just fifty yards of the wall is breathtakingly expensive and requires a crew of six working for half a year from a barge hired in Key West to float the bricks out. The annual budget for all such operations is only a fraction of what's required, but then that's the story of the modern Park Service. It takes some hundred thousand dollars' worth of diesel fuel to run everything here, from the air conditioners to the desalination equipment.

Meanwhile, more tourists, bristling with snorkeling equipment, are drawn in under the granite archway and down long, shadowy passages. In the bastion stair tower, they climb the triangular granite treads, which are arranged in a spiral on a central axis so that the fort's defenders could direct their fire more easily onto attackers. From the ramparts can be seen clouds of birds on Bush Key. The bird-watchers can tally as many as 103 species and are trying to do so with singular devotion. (One birder from Georgia, hearing of the presence of a red-footed booby, spent thousands of dollars to get here in a few hours so he could add it to his life-list.) The tourists, however, tend to end up in the visitors' center, looking at charts, iron door hasps, Enfield rifles, and pre-Columbian shell beads, and inadvertently learning of the fort's unlikely genesis and of what lies in view of the walls. What started out as a lark has become a lesson in natural and cultural history, with the inescapable conclusion that life in these climes has not always been sunscreen and margaritas.

THE DRY TORTUGAS were already well trodden when Ponce de León happened upon them in 1513. Seagoing prehistoric peoples from two continents had visited for as much as fifteen thousand years, and for two centuries after the Conquest, a rich mix of Calusa Indians, explorers, pirates, fishermen, turtlers, adventurers, unlucky sailors, and Key West salvers washed up here. In the last years of the eighteenth century, Thomas Jefferson arranged for a system of coastal forts to be built on the European model as a discouragement to those same Europeans. The last of these forts was on this deserted island at the mouth of the Gulf of Mexico, an ideal vantage from which to protect the fleet and commercial vessels in southern American waters.

Fort Jefferson was not begun until after Florida was acquired by the United States in 1841. Vast quantities of material and labor were transported with difficulty to this bit of sand. Fifteen years of labor by slaves was required to complete the lower tier, with casements for just some of the 450 big guns. Work continued during the Civil War, by Irish laborers brought from New York; deserters from the Union army were incarcerated at the fort while the architectural outline was completed, but the invention of rifled cannon, with its greatly increased destructive power, rendered the fort obsolete before it could see combat.

Fort Jefferson's most famous resident, Dr. Samuel Mudd, who had set John Wilkes Booth's broken leg after he murdered Lincoln, did hard time here before being released. The fort was abandoned in the 1870s, the frigate birds hanging in angular defiance of gravity above a not-quite-complete jewel of eighteenth-century military architecture, or a prime example of military overextension, depending on one's perspective. A quarantine station was set up, and a coaling dock built during the Spanish-American War. The *Maine* refueled in the Dry Tortugas before sailing for Havana and oblivion. The fort was used as a military outpost thereafter.

In 1935, President Franklin Roosevelt proclaimed Fort Jefferson a national monument. That didn't prevent the continuing plunder of its metal and cut stone over the decades, the destruction of the officers' quarters, or the tumbling of bricks into the moat, where they disturbed mostly smallmouth grunts and cruising moray eels.

One of Fort Jefferson's interpretive officers, a student of philosophy, had to learn the history and ecology of the Dry Tortugas on her own because the Park Service discontinued training. Rangers like her provide an invaluable connection between people and place, and she tells visitors, "Like castles in Europe, or the ruins in Central America, we should be proud of Fort Jefferson, a beautiful conch shell that happens to be empty. Try to imagine what it was like here—two thousand people, hot, without enough to drink, shooting at things." Millions of bricks were shipped from Pensacola, with incivilities between North and South interrupting that trade. Then the bricks came from New York, their deeper red evident in the upper tier of false casemates. Those in the ceilings were whitewashed to keep out rain and scorpions. "Here we have this fort saturated with human history, and the sea where nothing is human, and the wall like a psychological barrier between the rational and the primordial."

Some evenings, she walks out to the little campground outside the fort and recruits campers and pleasure boaters for a ceremony entirely of her own devising, part history, part theatrics. Using a collection of old clothes put together with the help of the Salvation Army, she costumes a few tourists, gives one the snare drum, and leads a march to the flagpole on the barricades. As the American flag is lowered, she plays the fife. "People cry," she says. "Some of them have been away from the States for months. This touches them."

The national parks were America's best idea, as a British ambassador commented a century ago; they have been compared to cathedrals, assembled by the polity using the scaffolding of politics. Unlike other federal agencies battling for funds, the Interior Department and the National Park Service within it possess some of the most spectacular real estate in the world and certified, irreplaceable treasures synonymous with the ideals of the country. And yet, elected officials who praise patriotism fail to preserve these embodiments of it. Politicians celebrate private enterprise at these public shrines without realizing that the separation of the two has been the parks' salvation.

The parks remain—though barely—some of the last places where citizens can escape the relentless merchandizing that has come to characterize contemporary life. Back in 1918, Secretary of the Interior Franklin Lane wrote to a Park Service superintendent on the subject of quality: "The national park system as now constituted should not be lowered in standard, dignity, and prestige by the inclusion of areas which express in less than the highest terms the particular class or kind of exhibit which they represent." It seems clear to me, surrounded by this massive artifice of nation building, and the artifice surrounded by natural perfection, both precarious, that the agency in charge requires more than bolstering.

I SLEEP FITFULLY on the deck of the Audubon Club boat and awake menaced by the shadowed openings of gun ports. The bird-watchers are off to search for American redstarts and myriad warblers, while I go visit the park's superintendent. He and his wife, the park's administrative clerk, were recently transferred here from Glacier Bay, Alaska. "In ways, the two places are similar in their demands," he says. "The same need to know a little bit about everything, the same remoteness and physical challenge." In his eighteen years in the Park Service, he has experienced an earthquake in northern California, a volcano eruption in Hawaii, and avalanches in Yellowstone. "When I arrived here, I thought, 'Now maybe I'll experience a hurricane.' And she said, 'Bite your tongue.'"

In September 1998, Hurricane George swept through.

"Thousands of birds arrived in the storm's eye from the Caribbean, exhausted. . . . We sandbagged the structures holding the generators, closed all the windows, and rode it out. But there was as much rain inside as out." Much the same thing happened with Katrina. Still, "visitation has exploded. People spill off these big boats, and more come on the seaplanes. The first thing they do is go to the head, and the bathrooms can't handle it. Some people tour the fort, but most of them just glance around and then hit the beach. They drop trash on the ground. We put out little pots with sand in them for their cigarette butts, and somebody tried to steal one."

Cuban refugees have also discovered the Dry Tortugas. On days when they arrive, the entire park staff has to turn out to deal with this latest contingent looking for a bit of America. So the invasion envisioned by Thomas Jefferson has been merely delayed and its nature altered. The new defenders who stick it out for two years have the right to transfer to the Everglades National Park, but some thrive on the daily rhythm here. The mechanic, for instance, happily keeps the seven generators humming plus the two tractors, a forklift, a mower, six boats, and other devices. In straw hat and beard, the mechanic looks like a latter-day Robinson Crusoe. He was previously on a nuclear submarine, and the isolation of the Dry Tortugas is nothing compared to living under the ocean: "No bikini babes down there."

Later, I see him pedaling between duties on a rusty bicycle. When one of the tires explodes in the heat, the ranger barges out of his quarters, strapping on his pistol.

THE TURTLE RESEARCHER, a lean, self-taught naturalist, spends twelve hours a day in the sun, checking for turtle kraals on the beaches. In his fifth season, he came originally as an AmeriCorps volunteer and now works with a patchwork of research grants and the kindness of fellow islanders. "I'm a kind of scavenger. I eat with one of the rangers and do his dishes in return. It's like a family on the Dry Tortugas, and not necessarily a happy one."

The interpretive officer diverts herself by painting pictures and reading horror stories "to get me through the long nights." She adds brightly, "I've had only two ghost-type experiences," one involving the mysterious unlatching of a window in her quarters, the other the sound of contending male voices in a remote, deserted section of the fort. "And often when I pass by Dr. Mudd's cell, I get this distinctly odd feeling," although the doctor had been released in 1869.

Folding chairs are arranged that night in rows under the weeping brick ceiling of a damp casemate. The kerosene lantern hanging above the corroded shutters throws a warm, nineteenth-century glow over the faces of the assembled visitors, mostly bird-watchers with scopolamine patches still behind their ears, happy with the day's "blowdown"—the forced landing of birds in a storm. This program is an appreciation of the variable nature of the Dry Tortugas, in which the human history is but a moment in the saga of evolution.

I am reminded of this when I return to the birders' boat and stand at the rail, looking down into depths illuminated by a single halogen lamp. Shrimp and fry swarm at the surface, while below them a big tarpon courses back and forth like a thick scimitar of quicksilver, gorging, his eye blood red in the reflected light. The proliferation of marine organisms here at the juncture of the

Gulf of Mexico, the Caribbean, and the Florida Straits affects the biological health of both Florida coasts. Oceanic gyres converge, concentrating and dispersing a great variety and profusion of life. The species include lobsters, snappers, groupers, grunts, wrasses, triggerfish, shrimp, conch, and innumerable microscopic creatures. This vital nursery to the deep, its reefs, sea grass meadows, and sandy bottoms, extends beyond the edges of the park's small, watery footprint.

Out there, commercial fishermen gather on the edge of one of the few fertile fishing grounds from which they can quickly motor to a safe harbor—the park's—and have dinner before returning to the take. The National Oceanographic and Atmospheric Administration has established a protected Tortugas Ecological Reserve just to the west, part of the existing Florida Keys National Marine Sanctuary.

SATURDAY MORNING, and the turtle researcher returns from checking the outlying keys where he will soon be observing turtles crawling from the surf to deposit their eggs. The habitat is ideal: no raccoons to eat the eggs, no rubble on the beaches to prevent their being laid, no lights to attract the hatchlings. But there are threats nonetheless, and not just fishing nets and boat props. "I see the visitor impact," he says. "I think if they don't change things here, they're going to lose it."

Another ferry is docking as we talk, its railings crowded with the visitors from Key West who have passed the coral atolls known as the Marquesas, and the lonely stretch of water, the Quicksands. They disembark in swimsuits and dark glasses, smelling of suntan lotion, and sure enough, long lines immediately form outside the restrooms.

Members of the Tropical Audubon Society have identified ninety-seven species, including a prime life-listing: the short-eared owl, on a jaunt from Cuba to feast on "Tortugas squirrels" (rats). Among the birders is a diminutive man in Bermudas and a baseball cap, a retired research biologist for the U.S. Geological Survey who worked in the Everglades for forty years and has been coming to the Dry Tortugas since 1956, when he spent his honeymoon here.

He takes a break from the movable ornithological feast and sits at a picnic table in the campground, with a view of the moat and the broad, blue sea. "The problem here isn't a shortage of sewage capacity," he says, following the arc of an orchard oriole, "but of upland area. That little clump of buttonwoods over there has forty or fifty species in it. The birds in the spring and fall migrations are insectivores, so you can't destroy the vegetation without running into major problems. . . . Migration is an evolutionary test. They have to fight the winds, and arrive here exhausted. Without food, you can have hundreds die."

He adds, "We're on the edge of a big change," and suddenly the condition of the fort seems a lot less pressing than the preservation of the place. "In a decade, the Dry Tortugas has gone from a place with few visitors and staff to a major tourist destination, as they say. The big question is, can the place, and the Park Service, react appropriately and in time?"

Chapter 9

CUMBERLAND ISLAND

A VERY DIFFERENT OCEAN WASHES THE BARRIER islands in the Atlantic off the southeastern coast. The celebrated American naturalist William Bartram passed within sight of this, the southernmost island off the coast of Georgia, more than two centuries ago on his classic journey through these climes. Later, the force of distant fortunes was felt here as in the Dry Tortugas but with a different cast and intensity: the wealthy outsider altering a landscape as well as a culture and then being supplanted by the federal government.

Today the traveler sees from a ferry what must have

greeted visitors a century ago: marsh grass, inland water-ways scoured by steely afternoon sunlight, a triumph of sedimentary geology and photosynthesis with some signs of human habitation. Mostly, there is deep shade thrown by the trees, where mosquitoes breed exponentially and feral hogs and horses coexist with deer and turkeys. I was struck when I first saw Cumberland by the sense of well-being, as if contentiousness and striving characterizing the mainland had been put off here by the isolation, rich natural beauty, and ambient ocean air. But that impression was illusory.

A sandy road tunnels through a hauntingly beautiful coastal biome to reveal a raised plantation-style house converted to an inn, surrounded by live oaks and palmettos, with associations antebellum and deeply Southern. The house, Greyfield, was built in 1901 by the industrialist Andrew Carnegie's more retiring brother, Thomas, who owned 90 percent of the eighteen-mile-long island. He and his wife, Margaret, had other houses built on Cumberland, including their forty-four-room, turreted residence, which burned in 1959.

Greyfield, however, was for their daughter, and the sitting room still serves as a kind of Carnegie reliquary: books with tattered covers, worn Oriental carpets, heavy furniture designed for ease, and a Remington-esque bronze of polo players. Ruled lines on the cypress wall, obscured by drapes, tell the heights of Carnegie heirs from the 1920s to the present. Thomas Carnegie's granddaughter is captured in a portrait revealing also the theatrical effect of wilderness on a flower of industrial royalty, her head bound in a scarf, gypsy style, and a knife on her belt.

The island's future was supposedly settled in 1972, when it was made a national seashore. But a few years later, a dispute arose over the island's biological and historic value and, specifically, the fate of yet another Carnegie house, Plum Orchard, and the wilderness surrounding it. The dispute carried implications for other properties in America also under the aegis of the National Park Service and eventually threw together a cast of park personnel, celebrities, environmentalists, and the Carnegie progeny who became implacably opposed.

More miles of sandy road lead to Plum Orchard, the classical revival mansion set on a broad lawn, fronted by two royal palms, with a bull's-eye window in the portico attic. A raised piazza with a balustrade extends along the front facade, grand and a little sad. "Plum," as they call the house on Cumberland, was built in 1898, the wings added later. Plum was built for the Carnegies' fifth son, George, whose wife was Margaret Thaw, sister of the notorious Harry Thaw, who in 1906 shot and killed the architect Stanford White. (White had been intimately involved with the lovely Evelyn Nesbit, who happened to be Thaw's wife.)

The house is more impressive by virtue of size than architectural distinction and reminded me, when I first saw it, of other grand expressions of accomplishment scattered around the South and built before the advent of income tax. Soon after Plum was acquired by the Park Service, also in 1972, it was assigned the "second order of significance," meaning it should at least be preserved. But twenty-five years later, the paint was peeling, the eave of one add-on porch had sagged, and the carriage house out back had collapsed. Everyone involved agreed that something had to be done about the rapidly deteriorating mansion, but how the house should be put to use, and at what risk to the wilderness surrounding it, were open questions.

CUMBERLAND ISLAND became known to many Americans when John F. Kennedy, Jr., was married there in 1996. The person arranging it, a friend of John-John's, was the slight, dark-haired, forty-five-year-old great-great-granddaughter of Thomas and Lucy Carnegie. When I meet her, Janet "Gogo" Ferguson is dressed in black leotards not entirely suited to wilderness and wearing silver jewelry of her own devising. "Coming here as a child," she says, "when it was all lit up, I felt it was a magical place."

The fourteen-karat gold bracelet mimics rattlesnake ribs, part of a line of commercial jewelry that also includes alligator scutes, gar and armadillo scales, and porpoise disk plates. Gogo describes herself as a poor relation who regularly visited Cumberland from Massachusetts as a child when Plum was a retreat for her and her relations and when nights were spent in the lingering light of the Gilded Age. "If we can save the house with a small group of people," she asks, "why not?"

It is a familiar question, but the answer's not as obvious as it appears. Gogo started a foundation, the Plum Orchard Center for the Arts, with the intention of making the house into a retreat for artists, writers, and dancers, and sought commitments for more than $10 million in outside donations. She placed on her board of directors such luminaries as a television anchorman, the wife of a famous novelist, another famous writer and

New York literary gadfly, and John-John Kennedy, now deceased. That was about as far as the artists' retreat had been taken.

A Park Service ranger joins us and unlocks the front door of Plum, and we all step into the foyer. The walls are hung with faded linen wallpaper, the tall windows draped against the sun; light from the fan window illuminates the massive fireplace. "This place has sentimental value for me," Gogo says, "but it is also very much a part of history, what Cumberland Island is all about."

In the library, we find a Tiffany lamp that belonged to Lucy Carnegie at Dungeness, cloudy amber glass in a turtleback pattern—"after the loggerheads," Gogo says, of the sea turtles that come to Cumberland every year. In the old days, the cabinets were full of shotguns, the walls hung with trophies. Dinners at Plum Orchard were formal, with butlers dressed in green livery. George Carnegie had left little but books, firearms, and saddles. Plum passed to his sister, and her husband's Cumberland Island exploits reflected more privileged, bizarre adventures—he once tied a live rattlesnake to a car running board. Then in the 1960s, a developer acquired the rights to some remaining private land on Cumberland and threatened to build a planned community. The Park Service bought him out and, at the same time, acquired other private holdings from the Carnegie heirs and others, some of it still in life estates. In 1971, Plum Orchard and twelve surrounding acres, plus $50,000, were donated to the National Park Foundation by the heirs.

In the master suite upstairs is an imposing bed set on a parquet floor. The bathrooms are large, with enormous showerheads and fine detail in the soap dishes, but the steam-heated towel racks have been cold for decades. Plaster has fallen in several rooms. The stove in the kitchen has rusted out. In the pantry, drawers marked "breakfast mats" and "luncheon napkins" suggest the high level of social organization in times past, but the white tiling around the indoor pool is cracked and the little wooden gallery above the squash court full of ghosts.

In 1982, Congress designated nearly half of Cumberland—8,800 acres—as official wilderness, with special restrictions on its use. Plum lay in the heart of it, and the house quickly became a symbol of the difficulty of administering de jure wilderness containing houses and roads and of what some say was the Park Service's reluctance or inability to assume responsibilities of this sort assigned to it by Congress. A wilderness management plan was never prepared, and Plum fell into disrepair. The appraisal for what was required just to bring the house back would have cost $150,000, money that the Park Service would have to raise. "This is a low priority," Gogo points out. "They need public-private financing."

In 1994, the Park Service and the Plum Orchard Center for the Arts had signed a memorandum of agreement whereby Gogo's foundation might take over Plum. Then some awkward questions were raised by environmental groups. What seemed to be an easy solution to Plum's predicament quickly became something else. The questions were pointed: What would be the effect of twenty artists and ten support staffers—nearly doubling Cumberland's full-time population of thirty-five—on the surrounding wilderness? How accessible would Plum be to other visitors to the island? And why should a relatively few people from a private foundation control the use of a fabulous public place?

The criticism came from several groups, among them the Atlanta branches of the Wilderness Society and the Sierra Club, but local mainland environmentalists were particularly outspoken. They filed a lawsuit to force the Park Service to draw up a wilderness management plan and conduct an environmental assessment. Because of the strength of the opposition, the Park Service withdrew from its memorandum of agreement and opened Plum Orchard to competitive leasing bids, as originally dictated by the National Historic Preservation Act.

The suggestion that the Carnegies' heirs could favor anything inappropriate to the island, as implied by the name Defenders of Wild Cumberland, clearly annoys the Carnegies' great-great-granddaughter. "Some people think this is some kind of grandiose plan of the rich," says Gogo, "but Plum represents five generations of my family. The critics should be glad they're not looking at another Hilton Head."

THIRTY YEARS AGO, a naturalist named Carol Ruckdeschel came to Cumberland Island. She had been the subject of a profile by John McPhee in *The New Yorker*. In "Travels in Georgia," McPhee wrote about her habit of collecting roadkill for research and occasionally for eating: "She was trim and supple and tan from a life in the open. Her hair, in a ponytail, had fallen across one shoulder." In one memorable scene, she held aloft a large water snake "like a piece of television cable moving with great vigor." The image was striking, as were the identities of her housemates: an injured red-tailed hawk, a rattlesnake named Zebra, and many black widows.

Ruckdeschel had begun to study sea turtles on Cumberland (McPhee, as it happens, had written about the island in his book *Encounters with the Archdruid*). She acquired a small house in which to work, in an isolated spot called the Settlement, which comprised a cluster of structures with a church and which had once been home to descendants of slaves. Under an agreement with the Smithsonian Museum of Natural History, she provided specimens from the creatures that washed up on the eighteen-mile Atlantic doorstep of Cumberland. Since her studies began in 1981, she had found 1,280 dead sea turtles—loggerheads, leatherbacks, Ridleys.

Hers is the only occupied house in the Settlement, one reflecting a preindustrial self-reliance (there is no telephone) fortified by forensic science and a vigorous rustic aesthetic: chicken coop and hog pen, bathtubs in the open air, the curved spine of a large mammal nailed over the door of a shack that serves as her laboratory, stumps of trees used to hold up the porch of the little museum she designed and helped build. "Two hundred years from now, Cumberland will be outstanding," Carol says, after I have taken a seat on her back porch. "We have to let the island restore itself, but right now, it's a mess."

The mess includes piles of boards to be recycled, odd bits of machinery, a vegetable garden, everything redolent of woods and barnyard, and the gently rotting carcass of a porpoise to be analyzed. ("Sorry about that.") She also means structures standing on other parts of Cumberland. Like hers, these structures are in life estates and will eventually revert to the Park Service and, theoretically, to the wild. The mess, she insists, does not include Plum Orchard. "The issue is not its preservation, but its use. The impact on the wilderness comes about through occupancy. If they just want to preserve Plum, that's doable. If they want to run a boat up here for a tour, there's nothing wrong with that. But people shouldn't be living there, with access to the wilderness.

"The whole issue has been twisted. We don't want to tear Plum Orchard down. I'm interested in cultural history, too. But the government should be working to reduce the number of people and vehicles on the island, to enhance wilderness values. The impact of people can only increase with this plan. Look ahead two hundred years, and you've got this node of activity smack in the middle of a wilderness area, a residential community that goes against everything the Park Service is supposed to support."

Fifty-five years old, she wears braids tied with blue and pink yarn, and a battered felt hat to which clothespins are affixed for holding the hair out of her face. She works as a freelance, self-taught biologist, mostly doing necropsies; the sun has weathered her skin since the days of *The New Yorker* profile, and her loose-fitting Levi's, rubber boots, belt, and knife scabbard are working gear, not the usual embellishments of temporary residents of still wild, sometimes difficult terrain.

She and Gogo Ferguson became friends soon after Carol first came to Cumberland; together they have gone through old Carnegie family diaries, looking for salient bits of natural history. But in 1994, Carol saw the Park Service's memorandum of agreement regarding

Plum Orchard and decided "the Park Service was shoving it under the rug." The plan's opposition by the Defenders of Wild Cumberland, which Carol helped found, angered many Carnegies. "I wrote to Gogo," says Carol, "and said I still love you like a sister. I don't hold grudges; this is just what I believe." She pauses. "Americans are so into ancestor worship that if we oppose this, they think we're against their family. They can't critically weigh alternatives. I'm not able to make the argument effectively to the family.

"This kind of artists' colony will bring the wrong kind of people to Cumberland, the rich and famous. They want conveniences. When John-John was married, why did the Park Service bring carloads of reporters through the wilderness, where they're only supposed to drive in an emergency? These administrators are worried about their annual ratings; they don't understand wilderness."

Meanwhile, she is collecting and cataloging, "saving all the ordinary things, like porpoises. It makes this very valuable because no one else is doing it. It's not an ooh-ahh collection; it's for research. If you're doing a study of, say, squirrels on the barrier islands, you could come here." This compendium of Cumberland wildlife—snakes, salamanders, fish in formaldehyde, whole turtle shells, the bones of storks and alligators—is all arranged on shelves, from small invertebrates to glamour species. The lab, likewise, is a jumble of projects, the most important a study of beach-combed turtles that Carol rightly believes have been killed by shrimpers who discovered them in their nets.

The kitchen has a woodstove. Carol prevents me from opening the refrigerator to get milk for my coffee, afraid I will be offended by the dead animals still kept there, not roadkill now but other vulnerable creatures. On the wall of her narrow study is a sign that expresses her ongoing concern: IT'S THE WILDERNESS, STUPID.

COMPROMISE SEEMS unlikely. Assertions by one advocacy group have elicited strong responses from the other. Carol sardonically calls Cumberland Island "the Carnegie National Monument," while Gogo criticizes Carol's "extremism and growing isolation." The lawyer for the Defenders of Wild Cumberland has described the prospective art colony as "just a bed-and-breakfast for the rich and famous out of the Northeast," while some Carnegie heirs have referred to environmentalists as "militants who come snooping around."

I try to imagine Plum Orchard animated by creative endeavor and intellectual intercourse, its fan window over the front door reflecting a fire in the massive ingle-nook off the foyer, pots steaming on a new stove, and a dance ensemble performing in the old squash court. Even Carol Ruckdeschel admits that to live near such a colony would be appealing. But the lawyer said, "Anybody can be an artist. To be very cynical about it, they could be doing anything in Plum under the guise of artistic activity."

When the Plum Orchard plan first became public, the director of the National Parks and Conservation Association had pointed out that the Park Service was "going to rely increasingly on public-private partnerships. Those partnerships contain incredible potential, as well as incredibly dangerous potential pitfalls for the parks." After years of management of the National Parks by the administration of George W. Bush, those pitfalls have multiplied and the harm done to the natural surroundings has become ever more apparent.

The Park Service had to protect both cultural and natural assets, and an action on one produced a reaction on the other. Occupying the house had an impact on the wilderness; similarly, allowing nature complete dominion meant the house's collapse. This difficult juggling act kept the questions levitated: Which comes first, history or nature? How far should the Park Service go in allowing foundations and other organizations access to national treasures, architectural and otherwise? What if Disney decided to assume responsibility for some larger national treasure, a Yosemite or a glacier? It seemed impossible at the end of the twentieth century, but not today.

The superintendent who originally signed the memorandum of agreement between the Park Service and the Plum Orchard Center for the Arts was transferred. The regional Park Service director for the southeastern United States in Atlanta chose not to talk to me about Plum. Indeed, various middle managers within the Park Service were clearly uncomfortable with the subject. Not so the former director Roger Kennedy: "The difficulties are those that were inherent in the formation of the park itself," he later told me. "Wilderness, private and public holdings, and historic structures. From the beginning these didn't lend themselves to easy solutions. The rhetoric tends to become absolute, and of necessity can't be."

Artists' retreats, he added, had a precedent in cabins

built in Rocky Mountain National Park half a century ago, and "resident artists were in consideration from the beginning, they were part of Stephen Mather's dream." (Mather was founding director of the Park Service in 1916.) The beneficial impact of wilderness upon artists was assumed, but no one had evaluated the converse.

Plum Orchard was listed on the National Register of Historic Places. The National Trust for Historic Preservation opposed the suit by Defenders of Wild Cumberland on grounds that the use of Plum and the attendant preservation were preferable to the house's demise. To the president of the Cumberland Island Historical Association, himself a Johnston and Carnegie descendant, Plum's use was immaterial as long as it was preserved. "My motivation is to see my family's home and furnishings made available to the American people," he said, not to establish an artists' colony. "If enough money could be raised to fix up and maintain Plum without it, no problem, but that's not likely to happen. So better the devil you know."

The devil turned out to be none other than the politicized federal bureaucracy of the early twenty-first century. The artists' colony went by the boards, and the Park Service introduced motorized sightseeing tours in passenger buses. Meanwhile, a local congressman on the mainland was trying to carve up the wilderness into separate pieces, opening the door for the very things the act protecting Cumberland Island was intended to prevent.

Chapter 10

GOD AND OLMSTED
IN WASHINGTON, D.C.

<hr/>

THE ROAD LEADS TO THE NATION'S CAPITAL BECAUSE so much of life in Cumberland, the Dry Tortugas, what's left of New Orleans, and the West depends upon it, and because Washington is the seat of government and the ultimate site of so many sacrosanct American institutions. Democracy supposedly thrives within the walls of the Supreme Court, the Capitol, and the White House, symbolized by them and by monuments to the first president, to Jefferson, Lincoln, and other proponents and defenders of the American experiment. All this is gently, and often brutally, subverted every day in a thousand interior spaces, many of them historic, by the nation's most gifted proponents of entitlement and self-interest. And the subversion still gets less attention than it should, despite the plague of scandal here and throughout the country.

The officially denominated architectural representative of God in the capital is the Washington National Cathedral, supposedly nonsectarian but in fact an adjunct of the Episcopalians, or, more precisely, of the Protestant-Episcopal Congregation. To the casual visitor, this, the last gothic cathedral to be built on earth, seems untouched by the harder realities of contemporary politics, including the reality that money in sufficient volume is irresistible.

The cathedral sits not exactly in my backyard, but close to it. For years I have looked up reflexively at the north tower, the temperament of its massed stone seeming to match my own, a chameleon effect of cathedrals noted by Henry Adams in *Mont St. Michel et Chartres* ("The cathedral has its moods"). Two of my three children—Brennan and Jessica—attended school within the confines of the cathedral grounds (the "close"), and I had seen the evolution of the cathedral from benign if powerful anchor of the city west of Rock Creek Park into an engine of tourism, development, and controversy.

The National Cathedral is only a century old, but seemed permanent; then one day I went for a walk inside with the man known as Clerk of the Works and discovered that it isn't. In the towering nave, looking up at the vaulted ceiling that resembled the interior of some mythic beast, its skeleton touched by polychromatic light filtered through stained glass, he mentioned erosion of the surrounding landscape, which had been designed by a son of Frederick Law Olmsted; the frailty of the altar rail, where visitors snapped off carved bracket ends for souvenirs; the deteriorating lead seams in the rose window; sagging sixteenth-century tapestries; and loose eyeballs in the equestrian statue of George Washington outside the south doors.

Cathedrals are for the displacement of earthly concerns by faith, which, like memory, often works best in familiar settings. But sustaining the physical presence of the cathedral is complicated by the demands of liturgy, church and local history, the elements, and of course human nature. Gravity accounts for what is simply called "the cracks," unobserved by hundreds of thousands of annual visitors, who do not suspect that the massive west facade is trying to pull away from the nave, as if the sandstone yearned for the quarries in Indiana from which it sprang. The south transept as well is tilting toward the Tidal Basin, the whole structure subtly Balkanized, a half a dozen separate entities built at different times all revealing their individuality.

In deserted spaces of the overcroft, above the boss stones of the nave, electronic devices measure minute movements and send impulses to a modem in a metal box that then transmits them to the U.S. Bureau of Mines in distant Pittsburgh. There they are analyzed by an agency accustomed to dealing with shifting mountains. Directly above the Holy Spirit Chapel, dark stains marked the nadir of a vertiginous leak that began far up under the north transept's acre of copper roofing. The magnificently carved choir stalls, pews, and peaked

doors throughout the cathedral have long been suscep-
tible to supplicants who leave behind hand oil and to the
cumulative effect of their passing garments. Wrought-
iron hinges, brass handles, needle-point kneelers all
suffer similarly. Meanwhile, pale, numinous light falls
through the stained glass onto a deserted scaffolding,
and Christ's parables are retold in more sober versions of
the ruby reds and striated blues, the basis of the medieval palette.

In 1898, a thirty-acre tract on Mount St. Alban, in
the relative loftiness of northwest Washington, was pur-
chased by the Episcopal Church as the site of a national
cathedral that had been under discussion for almost a
decade. Soon other tracts were added to comprise the
fifty-seven-acre close, and in 1907, the foundation stone
was laid in a ceremony attended by President Theodore
Roosevelt and ten thousand observers. English architects designed a traditional structure, although pressure
from disciples of modernism to abandon the gothic was
strong. The cathedral was subsequently completed in an
extraordinarily short time, there being no medieval wars
or monarchal rifts to deal with, and contained a total of
two hundred windows and 150,000 tons of limestone.
The demands of gothic detail constituted a universe
of artful opportunity, and problems. The wood alone
comprised a small forest of English and white oak, and
much of the carving was fine enough to defy replication
by American craftsmen.

The emblematic feature of this passion for detail in
wood was the screen on the south side of the Great
Choir, what amounted to a wall and gallery carved in
England and installed in the 1920s. Darkly burnished

and imbued with liturgical symbolism, the screen measured twenty feet high and eighty feet long, with legions of flowers, each blossom differing from those flanking it. Other carvings had not held up so well: fretwork on pointed doors, a broken acolyte's staff, an altar rail split by the weight of elbows, a succession of fractured brackets on rood screens, and deteriorating hymn boards and pew ends. The cathedral had tried unsuccessfully to find American carvers to replace the wooden piecework, and a representative even went to a duck decoy show on the Eastern Shore of Maryland in a failed attempt to find carvers. Now, two carving machines replicated the details.

Not so long ago, the cathedral employed twenty-seven full-time stone carvers to make eight hundred stone angels; now there is only one carver. Yet outside, hand-hewn stone is under assault by the sun and the continent's ever-shifting weather, and nowhere is this more apparent than on the heights, atop the central tower. Up there, past the huge bells, is a perch Saint Michael would have coveted. Mount St. Alban, the cathedral's terrestrial site, has a commanding view of the edifices of empire. The tower reaches up another six hundred feet, taller than the Washington Monument and planted with surveillance gear unofficially placed there by the intelligence establishment. The entire cathedral is subject to ferocious lightning, a condition that requires double cables of braided steel for grounding four spires. Below, the generous green of the cathedral close provides clear testament to the preciousness of open space in the city.

FREDERICK LAW OLMSTED, America's most famous landscape architect, died in 1903, a few years before work on the cathedral began. His sons, Frederick and Charles, had taken over the family firm and were designing parks and other cherished spaces for cities and suburbs, some of these in Washington, D.C. In 1901, Frederick Olmsted, Jr., had joined Daniel Burnham, Augustus Saint-Gaudens, and other luminaries to effect some elements of the city's original plan devised by the Frenchman Pierre L'Enfant, including the establishment of Rock Creek Park. In 1910, with construction of the cathedral under way, Olmsted was retained by the Protestant Episcopal Cathedral Foundation to come up with a plan for the grounds.

They were to include three schools and a liturgical college, as well as the cathedral. Olmsted suggested placing all these below the mount where the cathedral would stand and preserving most of the land as woods and open space. His idea was to make the close a transforming experience. "The great sweeping branches of the trees," he wrote, "seem to brush off the dust of the city, so that one at last reaches the Cathedral cleansed in mind and in spirit." He produced several plans, the last (in 1924) stipulating that only 14 percent of the close would ever be built upon.

This enlightened vision endured until 1998, when, in keeping with the times—the membrane of the twentieth century's second-most inflated speculative bubble had not yet burst—the cathedral foundation decided that Olmsted's building restrictions were onerous. The cathedral complex had what it euphemistically called "development needs," including a twenty-two-million-dollar, ninety-thousand-square-foot gymnasium with underground parking to accommodate 150 students of the exclusive National Cathedral School for Girls (NCS). This was to be not just any gymnasium for any school, but a facility to demonstrate the superiority of NCS, one of the best high schools in America, over its rivals in and around the nation's capital and, tacitly, over its gender equivalent on the other side of the close, St. Albans School for Boys.

Together these schools had shaped many of the nation's business and political leaders, among them George Bush, Sr., and Al Gore. No seventy-year-old blueprint by the son of a landscape architect from another century was going to thwart the fittingly determined, well-connected NCS board, even though violating the Olmsted plan would bring criticism. Hey, this was the supersizing era; fiscal and developmental restraint by those in charge of the country had been largely abandoned, and often debate along with them. The way to deflect criticism was to bury most of the new gym, cover the flat roof with sod, and declare it . . . a sports field! Thus could the building's two-thousand-square-foot imprint on the close be calculated at a mere 10 percent of its real size, and the cathedral and its associates could claim compliance with Olmsted's open-space requirements.

The cynicism of this decision caught those outside the negotiations, including many supporters of the cathedral, by surprise. The process that followed had far-ranging effects on the institution's relationship with the community and the perception of it, signaling "a change in program"—a fundamental shift of emphasis from spiritual to material concerns mirrored in other nonprofit institutions around the country.

One defense of the gym was its status as "state-of-the-art"—climbing wall, three full-sized basketball courts, a health club, and so on. Both gym and soccer field were someday to be made available to outsiders, for a fee. The notion that schools and other tax-exempt enterprises should give priority to profits and marketing, instead of mission, was still relatively new, but the cathedral was already receiving annually almost a million "pilgrims," the euphemism of choice for tourists who contributed millions of dollars to the general fund through donations, fees to charter bus companies, and purchases made in the shops.

The manipulation of the approval process for the gym would have done credit to the most ingenious, determined developer of Washington's commercial real estate, but then those were the ranks the cathedral had joined. As a religious institution, it wasn't bound by local design laws and took full advantage of this privilege. For a radical development in a residential neighborhood, all decisions were made in secret and the plans vetted by architects and attorneys well aware of the bare-knuckled expediencies of property enhancement. These hired experts ran out the clock in public meetings so that neighbors had little time to voice opposition, and effectively lobbied in the upper reaches of local and federal governments.

An environmental impact study, required by District of Columbia law for such a large project, was inexplicably waived at the last moment. Those opposing the gym were by now organized, and they learned that a powerful St. Albans alumnus who was publicly committed to a strong environmental ethic had been convinced to place a call to the mayor, the lesson being that school and tribal loyalties trumped all else. And the behavior of the NCS toward those of its own who opposed the gym was ugly.

Little of this received coverage in the local press. Many strings run from the Capitol and financial and lobbying institutions to Mount St. Alban; those with social, academic, and political connections to the close, including NCS's board of directors, rather than being cleansed in mind and spirit, had their competitive instincts honed and their ire raised by any objections. The neighbors put signs on their lawns imploring, "Don't throw us to the lions," and received anonymous letters of abuse. The cathedral's spiritual leaders remained aloof—"dithering clerics straight out of Trollope," as one of my neighbors put it—and deferred to the secular demands of their managers while the lawyers used a scorched-earth approach with the public. The "cathedral development needs" also included $100 million in new buildings for St. Albans' small student body and underground excavation in front of the cathedral to accommodate tour buses.

Excavation for the gym began in 2002, and over the course of months, heavy trucks carted thousands of tons of dirt from the city. A construction crane rose above the close, its skeletal profile and technological reach more striking than the cathedral's flying buttresses. The gym began to protrude from the ground—six feet on its western side, nearly twenty on the eastern—and in the process, an odd thing happened: The cathedral seemed to physically recede.

My own relationship with this process was complicated. I had spent many pleasurable hours in happy proximity to the close—on the St. Albans track, in the Bishop's Garden, in the cathedral itself. I didn't join the opposition, because I thought I might one day want to write about it, and yet the fight affected me and many people I knew, including some whose walls cracked and others whose basements were flooded after excavation began. I observed the unhappiness and desperation of those closer to the cathedral. These people saw their lives changing and felt a mounting sense of loss—both of space and of comity.

In shifting from tradition to profits, the National Cathedral has lost considerable moral authority, as well as inspirational value. These things are difficult to quantify but important, with broad social effects; once lost, they are not easily regained. The cathedral's public authority had become more legal than spiritual. Its demonstrated expertise in the exploitation of Washington's zoning laws and commercial opportunities seemed of more concern than did saving souls.

As for National Cathedral School, it seemed to me to have lost moral authority of a different sort: the absolute dedication to truth that such institutions should embody. By joining with an aggressive, development-bent board influenced more by a desire for showy architectural dominance than idealism, the school's administrators and coaches set an example diametrically opposed to the school's mission. The students, like the school's board and the cathedral's administrators, would eventually be gone, but not the dire effects of their brief tenure.

Abroad in the neighborhood, the cathedral had given up a century of nondenominational goodwill. With every tour bus added to the gauntlet, there was a proportionate drop in esteem. The roles of cathedral and "village" had been reversed: Those at the top had a view of the gym's sod roof—and of the shiny tops of cars delivering and picking up the students—that did indeed look like open space, while those lesser mortals beyond the close looked up past architectural clutter and a massive granite wall at the diminished symbol of salvation.

MUCH OF THE CITY is visible from Mount St. Alban, the walkway south of the flying buttresses affording a view of some monuments, including Washington's, and the Capitol dome. That white thumbprint of representative government placed so resolutely upon the fabric of city and nation also has an Olmsted connection. Arguably the most potent symbol of democracy anywhere, as well as a spiritual entity in its own right, the Capitol's natural surrounds were designed by Olmsted père and were undergoing a radical transformation similar in concept and process to what occurred at the cathedral, but with broader, more disturbing implications.

In 1873, Frederick Olmsted, Sr., who had profoundly influenced urban design in America, learned that Congress had, after years of bickering, agreed to enlarge the

Capitol grounds. Olmsted was asked to draw up a plan that would artfully pull the building and its surrounding fifty-seven acres together. He was to provide on the east side an entrance that was suitable for the representatives of the people and that would impress and reassure with its monumental heft. The landscape design is still one of the most important we have.

At the outset of the twenty-first century, workers began to take apart this same landscape, including the lampposts, lawn, and stately trees that had survived Washington developers for centuries. The deconstruction left, two years later, a fifty-foot-deep pit into which was to go a mere $265 million (at first estimate) underground visitors center. The new design incorporated not one, but two auditoriums (both the Senate and the House required their own, of course), two gift shops, a three-hundred-foot entrance ramp more reminiscent of Mussolini than Olmsted, and more interior space than the Capitol itself. The intention was to handle between three and four million annual visitors, who now waited more than three hours to enter the building, and to provide extra security for a Congress spooked by 9/11.

Olmsted scholars considered this draconian, grotesquely expensive project radical. Even though the Olmsted landscape was to be placed back on top like a vernal toupee, the ceremonial approach to the Capitol that living Americans remember would be gone. The architect at the Capitol was as little interested in community objections as he was in the opinions of scholars opposed to the plan, and unapproachable. Congress can—and will—do whatever it pleases, in this case with a truly iconic space not subject to the same reviews that other institutions receive in Washington. Worse, the historians working on the project had to sign confidentiality agreements, a first, to prevent discussion and delay. The project was soon behind schedule and well over budget.

There were remarkable parallels between this process and that at the National Cathedral, including closed discussions, stymied public debate, the alteration of carefully worked historic landscapes, and personal aggrandizement. The Cathedral School is a private institution, however, while the Capitol symbolizes the democracy that its current representatives subverted without apology.

If you were allowed to stand on the west side of the Capitol, on what is left of Olmsted's design, you would see in the distance more evidence of the arrogance of congressional power. Olmsted's original design was for a westward-facing Capitol, and he offered to design the Mall, then a partially realized, nineteenth-century tribute to the value of unencumbered land, as well, but Congress turned him down.

The Mall remains a triumph of sorts, although open space increasingly gives way to politics. There is no better evidence of this than the National World War II Memorial, dead in the center of the space, where familiar forces came together in defiance of the city, local interests, and scholars. All were again overridden by a Congress determined to build an uninspired trough between itself and a glowering Lincoln sitting in isolation at the far end. The memorial draws visitors, who wander in the heat of the sun reflected from stone, in a setting as reminiscent of Nuremberg as it is of Allied valor.

Relatively few visitors make it across the parkway to the memorial to Franklin D. Roosevelt, perhaps the most satisfying of all because of its natural repose, or that of Jefferson on the far side of the Tidal Basin. Grandly Palladian, emblazoned with the third president's words and biblical quotations, this tribute is sidelined, as if Jefferson were as offensive to the current opponents of reason in Congress as he was to those of his day. This architect of freedom is further cosseted by an ugly welter of barricades and chain-link fences, backed by the usual urban confusion of gritty highway, exit ramps, and railroad tracks.

The Potomac River lies beyond, affected by the tides and so a link to the sea, however distant; just across the river lies Virginia, birthplace of so many American rights, as well as Jefferson's doomed notion of a vibrant, enduring agrarian class as independent as it was industrious. I can't help but wonder if the third president imagined the loss of so much of his country not just to corruption and incompetence among the rulers, but also to large institutions supposedly dedicated to its preservation.

Chapter 11

NANTUCKET

MANY WASHINGTONIANS MAKING DECISIONS ABOUT
the city and the culture do not live there, or if they do,
they spend the more unpleasant seasons elsewhere;
Martha's Vineyard and Nantucket, both in Massachusetts, are seasonal extensions of Georgetown, K Street,
and even the Hill. Of the two, Nantucket is the most
difficult to reach and exhibits the greater clash between
tradition and the needs of America's new leisure class.

Ideally, Nantucket should be approached the first
time by sea, but the North Atlantic was a menace at
the time I wanted to visit the island, and so I booked a

seat on a propeller-driven plane leaving from Boston's Logan Airport. My fellow voyagers in the narrow waiting room included a tourist couple with matching luggage for a destination older than the republic itself; a handsome, middle-aged Nantucket resident with her hair pulled back and carrying a canvas crew bag instead of a suitcase and wearing shoes impervious to weather; and a forty-something couple displaying the contained impatience of the serial householder. The impatient woman's fashionable Anorak was cut for the silhouette, and she spent the minutes before boarding telling the tourists that she and her husband lived in New York but had "a place on the island," while her husband contemplated the tarmac. His clothes were a palimpsest of the privileged male's itinerant life: boating shoes, a many-pocketed rain shell, and on his head a billed cap stitched with the word *Montana*.

We all flew out over the coastal plain of eastern Massachusetts and into the vast, monochromatic veil of sea and sky. Nantucket was thirty miles away, a fourteen-mile crescent of sand and moors, jack pine, and spruce nicknamed "the gray lady" for the sober profile. Air travel allows us to grasp the geographic totality of such a setting as we approach, but at the same time deprives us of the impact of the unknown common to early seafarers who settled a very different America. The sere, weathered houses added to the island's beauty, windows reflecting what must have been spectacular views, but it was the fifty miles of unspoiled beaches, a white sand garland, that made the strongest impression from above.

The beaches were vulnerable to the elements, as was

the palpable evidence of America's past in priceless early American architecture taking shape as the plane came in: Cape Cod saltboxes and larger renditions built by Quakers, grand Federal and Greek Revival homes in town. Roughly twelve thousand people lived here, but the ambience of a lovely place out of time drew another thirty thousand seasonal residents. There were a quarter of a million day-trippers, who in summer rode the ferries or arrived by air, drawn by a combination of natural beauty and surviving architectural ambiance.

All this had drawn me, too, aware of Nantucket only secondhand and intrigued by the possibility that a famous American remnant had survived more or less intact. The little airport belonged to an earlier era, the runway free of the hundreds of private planes that park there in summer and make it the state's second busiest. I watched the couple with a place on the island go off in a car with a sticker on the bumper that said ACK, the airport's call letters and a sign they belonged.

I was taken into town to the Jared Coffin House, once the residence of a prosperous Nantucketer who had owned ships and candle factories. There were no streetlights and no franchised restaurants. The nation's infancy could still be touched—cedar shakes, wooden downspouts, hand-wrought timbers, and street cobbles brought as ballast in the old whaling vessels. The hotel's staircase creaked appropriately. I had dinner in the dim basement tavern, which was equally populated by the few visitors on the island and by locals. The tavern regulars reminded me of the tavern scene in *Moby Dick*, when Nantucket was a prime departure point for the earthly unknown, its founders dissenters, husbandmen, and entrepreneurs, mostly refugees from the Puritan mainland, and mostly Quaker.

Nantucketers refused to fight in the Revolutionary ("American") War, and their names included Macy and Folger, names that would become eminent in American commerce. Their commons system had assigned to each family shares of land and a say in the management of the island's resources. As an early observer, J. Hector St. John de Crèvecoeur, wrote in 1781, in his *Letters from an American Farmer,* "This happy settlement was not founded on intrusion, forcible entries, or blood, as so many others have been; it drew its origin from necessity on the one side and goodwill on the other."

Quaker rigor and simplicity had its contradictions, including some slave owning and contention among families for social and economic supremacy. But society also included whaling captains and the progeny of slaves who became fine seamen. The value of whale fat—America's first oil boom—precipitated a boom on Nantucket, too, a remarkable early American success story.

Before the Civil War, Nantucket was a typical border town, if sea-bound, and, due to merchant shipping, a preindustrial hub, its citizens thoroughgoing capitalists and its streets paragons of architectural inspiration. The houses symbolized achievement, as they do today, but Nantucket's contrarian streak had equal provenance. The island was the first community in Massachusetts to ban slavery and the first to integrate its schools, and it served as a stop on the Underground Railroad.

The discovery of oil on the mainland put whaling into a steep decline after the Civil War; the resulting depression on Nantucket lasted a century. By the late 1950s, Nantucket was a literal backwater with a barely surviving scallop industry and few tourists, its buildings and natural assets preserved mostly through inadvertence.

THE NEXT MORNING, I walked down to the harbor. In summer the water is thick with hulls and tenders full of day sailors and groceries. Hundred of boats awaited moorings, their owners' chances of joining the Nantucket Yacht Club almost nonexistent. Every evening in season, the club's commodore or vice commodore strode into the dining room a minute before sunset, said, "All rise!" and outside the club cannon was fired, Old Glory lowered, and then everybody sat down again.

Some knowledge of local usage is helpful on Nantucket. For instance, a "bug" is a little lighthouse, a "wart" a room added to a saltbox, a "cat-slide" a steep roof keeping the North Atlantic out of the oatmeal and trundle beds. A "Quaker four-bay" is not an overweight member of the Society of Friends but a house with three front windows and a door flush on the street. "Wash-ashore" applies not to driftwood but to residents who were not born on the island, and once a wash-ashore, you are one forever. "Reds" are not communists but pink trousers worn by some of the men, usually wealthy wash-ashores, and "lightship baskets" are no longer the make-work of operators assigned to the bugs in the nineteenth century for carrying lunch, but expensive purses owned by the wives of wash-ashores wearing reds.

The old-line Sankaty Golf Club was off-limits to most, including even visiting American presidents, but a new Nantucket Golf Club was offering access to its links for a mere $325,000 entrance fee. In season, any visitor to Main Street would see the faces of the owners of fashion houses, sports teams, and cosmetics companies. These newer rich were accommodated by representatives of money of a slightly older sort—the ranking officers of larger corporations—and these in turn were tolerated by the beneficiaries of inherited wealth, of whom there were many on the island.

Sprinkled throughout was a U.S. senator already running for president, and movie, music, and other media wash-ashores with a wide range of achievement, from television personalities to writers. Beneficiaries of the deflated bubble in technology included the head of an international company who would be convicted of fraud when tried. A brassy publication, N (for *Nantucket Times*), asserted that his "pals from Nantucket—along with a few from off-island—pledged over $30 million in property and other personal assets" should their pal need assistance meeting bail.

There were other currencies, however. "Money-making obsesses the nation now, out of the hegemony of the corporation, but there's a limit to what money can achieve on Nantucket," said a reflective Bostonian with a place on the island. "Architecture, and place, are being preserved. Despite the disparities in wealth, there's real community here at a time when that is threatened everywhere."

I found the two drugstores side by side on Main

Street, both in historic buildings, each with its own devoted clientele. Belonging was clearly prized, subtly achieved; Nantucketers might tolerate a felony charge, but not rudeness. CIVIL BEHAVIOR MANDATORY exclaimed the sign at the recycling center. But big new houses, and old ones jacked up for better views, had been radically altered behind their historic facades to accommodate powder rooms and dueling kitchen ranges, and resistance to outward change could be measured by the confusing array of nonprofits in the telephone directory.

Back in 1982, voters had dedicated 2 percent of all real estate transactions on Nantucket to a public fund for acquiring land to be set aside from development, the only such a law in the United States. Another prevented the destruction or significant alteration of the shapes and facades of historic houses. This had slowed the tear-down dynamic but did not prevent wealthy newcomers from building big new architectural statements on expensive plots. The new structures stressed the island in ways similar to those of the bygone whaling era: excess wealth and social ambition, logistical problems— getting materials, machines, and labor across open water—and a scarcity of housing for working people.

Also on Main Street I found the office of a fair-haired young man wearing Dockers and two shirts. He had built affordable half-duplexes, but had not had an easy time getting permits, blaming "people who get up at the town meeting and complain about development." This was early in George W. Bush's deregulated, soon-to-be deficit-ridden America. "Socialism hasn't worked anywhere in the world. What makes them think it will work on Nantucket? This isn't Cuba!"

Another sort of developer lived in a restored eighteenth-century cottage on India Street. He wore a round-collared linsey-woolsey shirt, period felt vest, and Birkenstocks; his wife wore a calico frock, her lemony hair in a ponytail. Together they pursued a combination of work and pleasure in various locations, among them Vermont, where they had just restored a historic hotel. At that moment, they had two construction crews working on Nantucket, and we went off in their Jeep Cherokee to see one of these speculative renovations. His family had been summering on Nantucket since the 1920s, and in the early 1990s, he and his wife had bought a Craftsman-style bungalow. Since then, they had bought eight more properties.

Two young men, neither of them Nantucket residents, were cutting trim on sawhorses. The couple had paid $950,000 for the house the year before, were putting $500,000 into it, and planned to sell it for $2.2 million. The deeply hued paints, bright window panes, lustrous floors, and, outside, a raised bed within a new stone wall faintly suggestive of another coast conspired in a happy amalgam of history and convenience, but I wondered what the original inhabitants would have thought of the house had they passed by on some heritage tour for the long departed.

ABOUT HALF THE remaining open space on Nantucket couldn't be built on, because the development rights have been bought. Ordinary citizens who worked for the town and county—the same thing on Nantucket—couldn't afford to buy a house here, and in many cases even to rent. The median price then was about $800,000; half the sales were for more than $1 million, and a quarter exceeded $2 million. All those figures have risen significantly. The haunts of locals on Main Street were closing because the owners lost their leases and watched those spaces become transformed into commodity shops, galleries, and expensive restaurants.

Schoolteachers vanished in summer, their houses and apartments rented for thousands of dollars a week to tourists; carpenters and plumbers rode over on the ferry from the mainland. The character of the island was changing because so many workers commuted. "You no longer bump into the person in the supermarket to whom you pay your cable bill," I was told by the editor of the *Inquirer and Mirror* ("The Inky Mirror"), Nantucket's weekly, which is now housed in a former gas station. "Workers show up on the dock at six-thirty every morning with an Igloo cooler and don't spend a dime on the island."

The needs of part-time owners provided much of the available work on Nantucket, but listen to just one of their stories: "You have to wait for weeks to get the simplest job done, and when they come, it costs a fortune." This from a psychiatrist who lived in Washington, D.C. "We had a leak and managed to get a roofer. He sat up there for most of the day, and when he came down, he handed me a bill for seven thousand dollars. To replace a few shingles! I wanted to take it to court, but my lawyer on the island said, 'Forget it, you'll lose.'"

Other than Williamsburg, Nantucket was probably the most heavily recorded town in America, but gut rehabs, teardowns, and new construction imperiled the island's identity. Destruction done to the interiors of the old houses in effect made a facade of the authentic, beggaring the notion *historic*.

It took me two days to find the director of the Nantucket Preservation Trust. Her name was Pat Butler, and she sat in a cramped office over a boutique, a slight woman in black jeans and bulky sweater. "The change in scale here is the most damaging thing to the culture," she said, the period windowpanes behind her streaked with rain. "Big new houses, big seasonal crowds. Then this place is a stage set, the people who live and work here hidden behind it." The year-round community was more "Dickensian. Everybody knows everybody else; we all feel we can endure the three months of summer for the quality of life the rest of the year."

It sounded more like Hawthorne to me. As a former member of the powerful Historic District Commission, the official body that rules on changes proposed for historic structures and on the style of new ones, Butler had created controversy by consistently opposing development. This had led indirectly to her being appointed head of the Preservation Trust by the Washington lawyer who had founded it along with a well-known Boston architect. Both men were wealthy longtime wash-ashores concerned with preservation, yet both had built controversial homes on the island.

The architect's house suggested a Quaker farmstead on a formerly untouched, windswept cliff overlooking

the sea, but it was, in fact, a string of structures con-
nected by a continuous, trenchlike basement containing
all the unseen support for the thoroughly contemporary
life, the "barn" a sleeping quarters and garage space, the
"house" a single room designed for living and entertaining, the connecting "tool room" a glass-walled kitchen,
most of which had required exceptions to zoning
ordinances.

The lawyer's architectural endeavor had caused even
more comment. Married to a grocery chain heiress with
a well-known pastry named after her, he had first torn
down an old house on the beach in town to build the
new one, described by Pat Butler as "drop-dead beautiful" and brimming with antiques, scrimshaw, period furniture, and art. But "the old house was familiar, loved,
iconic." The Historic District Commission had granted
permission to tear down the old one, and Butler now
regretted taking part in that decision. "The new house
became another sort of icon—of great wealth acquiring historic property and leaving behind a twentieth-
century identity."

She had fallen out with the Washington lawyer and
the Boston architect, both of whom were no longer
affiliated with the trust. She lived on the grounds of an
eighteenth-century center hall colonial that had once
belonged to a whaling captain. The house was for sale
with strict limitations on what could and could not
be done to the house by any buyer, including interior
changes. Pat took me to see the house, which had a fan
window over the center door and, inside, "clear-ways"
over the doors—panes of old, flawed glass that had

allowed "peeping," Butler said, "and prevented people from feeling alone." The clear-ways also provided early detection of accidental blazes in adjoining rooms, and some light in long winter months touched by a cold, low-angled sun.

Under the hearth supposedly lay the sail from the founding captain's whaling vessel, although a buyer would probably not be allowed to remove the wide, worn floorboards. The last owner, deceased, had been a friend of Butler's and considered herself the house's steward. She had wanted the restrictions, and the house had become something of a test case. Would it sell for a great deal of money when the facade, interior walls, colors, even shelving, couldn't be changed except through appeal? Tax advantages for the buyer would be calculated on the difference between what the house was worth without restrictions, and with them, giving some financial incentive to those willing to hamstring their redecorating impulses.

I tried to imagine the house inhabited by the couple I had seen on the plane, now sojourners in history, he hanging his *Montana* cap on a peg and taking a hard chair before the fireplace, next to his wife. Would she be content with the simple realities of the narrow kitchen and guestrooms at the top of the house without bath or privacy? Would they serve wine and smoked salmon from town to weekend guests, or home-made beer and Indian pudding? Theirs would be a museum existence literally infused with the past, and unique. But would the restrictions rankle after they had paid five million?

THE INTENSITY OF the committed life on Nantucket, whether Dickensian or Hawthornian, seemed to me to pose problems of accommodation on a small island. For some guidance, I went to Nathaniel Philbrick, author of a popular book about the whaling ship *Essex* and others, and formerly a sailing journalist who had moved to Nantucket with his wife and become a historian. He agreed that restrictions were inherent in Nantucket's past and present. "The Quakers had committees for everything," he said, over a sandwich in the Jared Coffin House, "getting married, saving a failing business, building a house." Early Nantucket was emblematic of the nation. "Sand banks provided a clean slate," he said, upon which were written the rules of close association.

The success of whaling cut into that solidarity. Many cultures had washed up on the shores, including Quakerism. "We're seeing evidence of the same thing today: Each generation assumes this is an Eden, and people come expecting that." Now Nantucket's real estate and industry were largely in the hands of wash-ashores, not locals. Its land and architecture were subject to exacting controls, but the building and the influx of wealth continued. "Some change is good," said Philbrick, "but at what point do you ruin what is here?"

Back in the 1960s, the island had been taken up by a developer who saw it as a prospective destination of the wealthy long before anyone had ever heard of heritage tourism or the Internet. His name was Walter Beinecke, and he made the famous assertion that Nantucket did not want the sort of visitor "who arrives in a dirty T-shirt, with a five-dollar bill, and changes neither."

Still a controversial figure on Nantucket, Beinecke had bought up waterfront property in town and not quite single-handedly prevented an influx of salt-water taffy shops and other businesses catering to sunseekers and partiers. He and a handful of friends and investors who had traditionally summered on Nantucket also launched the Nantucket Conservation Foundation, which bought up development rights to open space and helped to preserve the look and feel of a unique place, even as these people tastefully exploited the rest of it.

I assumed Beinecke was dead, but would later discover him quite alive, not on Nantucket but in Newburyport, New Hampshire, a depressed coastal town where he was attempting to replicate what he had done on Nantucket half a century earlier. The day I arrived at his condo, his wife went off to lunch and left us at the kitchen table. Physically frail, Beinecke sipped juice from oranges shipped up from his place in Florida and talked.

His grandfather had founded H&R Green Stamps, he said, providing his heirs with early economic advantage. In the late 1940s, Beinecke bought a summer place on Nantucket for $12,000 (which he sold in 2001 for $12 million). "I couldn't understand why the place was still depressed," he said, of 1940s Nantucket. "Even Roosevelt's arsenal of democracy failed to reach its shores." The island began to attract tourists—actors, artists, academics—as well as the day visitors. Beinecke decided to develop Nantucket as a kind of hobby. He went to a New York real estate developer, who gave him crucial advice: *shopping*.

"Shopping was no longer a necessity, but a potential pleasure," Beinecke said. "But a place needed attractive shops and prosperous shoppers. Nantucket had three populations at the time—natives, summer folk, and 'trippers,' also called 'mangies'"—the tourist in the dirty T-shirt. Beinecke set out to eliminate the mangies. "Cape Cod had the same things to offer, and the Cape didn't require a trip to an island. We would have to find something different."

That something was "distinction. It makes people pay more for things." Nantucket had many possibilities for distinctiveness: natural beauty, history, architectural excellence. Preservation of these things was the way Nantucket could capitalize, he thought, "as a peddler, but that meant the clientele would have to be limited, so as not to destroy the character."

Real estate was cheap. "People were lining up to sell, and Nantucket had no zoning code or preservation standards. You could do anything." He bought scallop shacks, had them put on the National Register, and then moved them back from the water and rented them to artists. He rented shop space only to "nuts—dedicated types. I didn't want the guy who went to trade shows to pick up his inventory, but one who went home to Czechoslovakia, say, and brought back something of distinction. I wanted a woman who knew fashion, a nut with distinction. I didn't care if she was right or wrong."

He realized that getting to Nantucket required real yachtsmen, and that they would want to moor near real fishermen. "Within a couple of years, we were getting yachts from Europe—one had a helicopter, another an open fireplace, another separate davits for a Chris-Craft tender and a Volkswagen." Merchants realized they could sell three $300 sweaters a week to such people. McDonald's wanted in, "but we had enough real estate to control the situation." He bought the White Elephant guesthouse, which had been owned and run by a woman who "met people at the door in black silk lounging pajamas and served tea off a casket." She sold the guesthouse to Beinecke for "ten thousand dollars and a case of gin." Beinecke tore it down and built a new hotel with the old name.

By 1980, his vision had paid off, and he sold out to a real estate syndicate. "Now they're building on the moors that ought to be open. They're killing the golden goose."

I LATER TALKED to the head of the municipal employees union about the downstream effects of Walter Beinecke's vision. She denounced in a gravelly voice "people who have plenty and don't want others to get theirs." These so-called IGOMs ("I've got mine") thought they could control further development with legislation, "but market forces have always been at play here."

She didn't object to new buildings, because they meant, among other things, revenue for the town and more efficient office space. "The trophy homes during the Quaker era looked awful to other people then, too. It's cyclical. But the outside world is much closer now," she added, contradicting herself a bit, as islanders sometimes did. "The ferries are faster, in summer the alcohol and drug arrests fill the newspaper. Summer people ignore the stop signs; they think this is utopia. Their maids and au pairs commute by plane. The people who live here are close-knit, but the minuses are beginning to outweigh the pluses."

I went to a dinner party and heard the usual stories: an impending lawsuit over the proposed development of a bog; the local maritime museum spending an inordinate amount of money on a party to celebrate its own success; the famous writer who lived seasonally on Nantucket denied a table at the White Elephant—all unthinkable a few years ago.

As I was walking back to the hotel, I saw in the warm light of curtained windows a preindustrial illusion both powerful and oddly saddening. The island was undoubtedly beautiful, a jewel of past architectural brilliance, but was not an exemplar of an enduring way of life the structures represented. There was community, but dominated by drop-in citizens whose real concerns, like their livelihoods, were elsewhere.

As in so much of America today, the notions of place and home were subsumed in privileged itinerancy and greatly affected simply by the showing off of money. Thus two dedicated preservationists—the Washington lawyer and the Boston architect—tore down a historic house to replace it with a modern one and radically altered enduring maritime landscapes. But these were minor infractions compared with the damage wrought by some serial householders.

The American virtues that the island had once so colorfully represented—independence, risk, hard work, sharing, symbols of a bygone national purpose—were largely missing, or as meaningless as corporate slogans. Like the lovely eighteenth-century facades, such words concealed self-regard and technological distraction from present-day reality. Meanwhile, the scallop boats were curiosities, and old Beinecke's shopping imperative had taken over everything from historic sheds to marketable views.

THE PERSON WITH the longest view of Nantucket's future was not an activist, a politician, or a homeowner, but a scientist in charge of the University of Massachusetts's Nantucket Field Station. He was conducting a study of the effect of waves and currents on the island, and reminded me that fifteen thousand years ago, there was dry land between Nantucket and the mainland: "In geologic terms, I'd give this alluvial island four hundred years, with the current rate of erosion and the rising sea level."

The Jared Coffin House, the whaling captain's residence, the White Elephant, the architect's faux Quaker homestead, and all those carefully maintained facades stood on "the last surviving piece of the Nantucket shoals that is leading with its sandy chin into the waves of the north Atlantic."

Chapter 12

UP IN MAINE

We are paddling on wind-hazed water, at the top of the eastern seaboard, in another century. Spruce, jack pine, and balsam cozen the shore of this drinkable lake, an unbroken expanse of green under a cloud-streaked sky that is both broad and intimate. Floating below us, the inverted reflection of Spencer Mountain is scored by the long, straight wakes of two cruising loons.

Maine, for me, was synonymous with the outdoors and mostly beyond the reach of the ambitions transforming Nantucket and elsewhere. It also recalled the ramblings and writings of Henry David Thoreau, author of *Walden* and the assertion, made in a time before cell phones, that people lead lives of quiet desperation. But Thoreau also wrote *The Maine Woods,* a book that captured a different place and different sentiments. When I read this story of the wild north country, it made me want to see a moose knee-deep in a tea-colored river and discover other remnants of a landscape that profoundly moved this, the most famous of American nature writers.

A few hours earlier, I stood in a barn down in Willimantic, Maine, with a handful of other pilgrims. "There aren't too many 'don'ts,'" Garrett Conover told us. "Don't use the ax. Don't talk to us during dinner prep, and don't relieve yourselves less than two see-fars from the water." A see-far is the distance you can see into the woods while standing on the bank. "There's no giardia where we're going. You don't want to go down in history as the one who introduced it."

He wore a belt with a moose etched into the buckle. His beard was reminiscent of Thoreau's, his gaze fixed on a point several see-fars in the distance. His wife, Alexandra, stood next to him in a battered Stetson, a scarf, and a wool vest; both sported the familiar Maine guide shoe, really a rubber boot with a leather upper. Their barn was loaded with traditional expeditionary gear: a sixteen-foot birch-bark canoe made in the style of the Penobscot Indians, snowshoes of bent ash and rawhide, and pack baskets of beaten ash strips they made themselves. A dozen "blanks" of drying ash hung in a side room, to be carved into paddles with a traditional north woods crooked knife.

The rest of us look considerably less Thoreauvian

in floppy hats and rip-stop nylon jackets, all of us "from away," as they say in Maine: my grown daughter, Susanna, an artist; Robyn, a social worker from Manhattan; Svea, a retired nurse from Concord, Massachusetts, Thoreau's home; Svea's granddaughter, Sofia, nine years old, half American, half Italian, from Bologna, in pink boots; a professional photographer, Jim, from Kansas; and me, a writer from the environs of the nation's capital, quietly desperate to escape them in July.

We had all received the same letter from the Conovers, telling us what sort of trip to expect. "If you are reluctant to part from radios, cell phones, satellite phones, and your laptop computers, please seriously consider *not* participating. . . . Much of the magic in wildlands trips comes from engagement with the present, with natural conditions, and with the temporary tribe of each group."

OUR TRIBE IS NOW about to camp on Lobster Lake. We quickly learn the setup dance: canoe unloading, tent site selection, tent erection, and, finally, body immersion. The lake is cold enough to get even a Mainer's attention. "Step into my office," says Svea after the swim, and we take turns sitting with her at a picnic table provided by the Maine Department of Forestry, for pulse readings. She is learning about "plant spirit," and explains, "I would like to take each of your pulses every day. The Chinese say that's an integral part of the healing process." I doubt that Thoreau would have been sympathetic to the notion of plants having spirits, despite his transcendentalism, but he would have found it interesting and no doubt would have recorded the experience.

Thoreau made three visits to north-central Maine—in 1849, to climb Mount Katahdin, and in 1853 and 1857 to the headwaters of the Penobscot and Allagash rivers. Along the way, he encountered hunters, loggers, and other explorers and passed through a continuous forest that seemed inexhaustible. He took notes about plants, birds, mammals, and other natural phenomena and commented on things as various as the stars and the destructive habits of his fellow human beings. He wasn't after financial gain or sport, but knowledge, valuing wilderness not for its product but for the inspiration and wisdom it could impart to his generation and future ones.

I am confident that he would have documented the Conovers' cooking routine as well, had he been with us. Garrett has fetched spruce while Alexandra arranged the pack baskets and food boxes (*wanigans*). He cuts foot-long logs with a bow saw assembled for that purpose while she sets two poles in the ground, lashes the galley pole between them, and suspends buckets on chains. Garrett expertly splits the logs with a fine Swedish ax, produces a flurry of wood shavings and then a crackling fire; Alexandra has the biscuits in motion. He makes a pot of his "decapitated" (decaffeinated) coffee while she peels potatoes and gets the steaks ready. He assembles out of a canvas case a skillet eighteen inches across, and she prepares the salad.

"Around here, the name Thoreau brings a groan," she is saying. "When he came through in 1857, he refused to exchange news of the outside world with a family living at the portage to the Allagash. Thoreau just took off down the trail, and then he got lost. The story was picked up by all the guides in the Chesuncook region, and they have long memories. I heard it from our mentor, Mickey Fahey, who heard it from his, Tommy Smart, who heard it from a guide who was alive at the time."

The tradition of the official Maine guide goes back to 1897, when they were accredited by the state to promote the beauty of Maine and to assure clients from points south that the forests, lakes, and rivers were user-friendly. The first guide was a woman, six-foot Cornelia "Fly Rod" Crosby, who wrote a newspaper column and convinced one of the railroads operating in Maine to send her to a sportsman's convention in New York's Madison Square Garden with a genuine log cabin and a stuffed moose. So Alexandra is part of an old tradition, but Maine woods lore is much older, and it is the early traditions that got the Conovers interested in making their own pemmican and moccasins sewn from smoked deer hide, and in natural pursuits not related to hunting and fishing. They began their apprenticeships fresh out of college in Massachusetts more than twenty years ago, with liberal arts degrees and a desire to study under the legendary Maine woodsman Mick Fahey. "Garrett and I were already competent outdoors people," Alexandra points out. "Then Mick asked me if I wanted to learn to paddle. I was insulted."

Fahey had learned his skills from Smart and from members of the Penobscot tribe he encountered as a younger man. Among other things, he taught the

Conovers to put their bodies into forty to sixty strokes a minute, with a paddling style and rhythm used by American Indians, trappers, and voyageurs of an earlier age. The technique is known alternately as the Maine stroke, the Canadian stroke, and the north woods stroke. Fahey taught them much more—"not just to question but to understand nature—astronomy, limnology, forestry. We got so much from him and other old-timers. They opened windows that led to everywhere."

Garrett later wrote the ultimate treatise on poling canoes, *Beyond the Paddle,* and together he and Alexandra wrote *Snow Walker's Companion.* Neither of these is in the camp library—a clear plastic bag—but I do find *A Canoeist's Sketchbook,* by Robert Kimber; *The Book of Swamp and Bog,* by John Eastman; *The One-Eyed Poacher and the Maine Woods,* by one Edmund Wayne Smith; and *The Wildest Country: A Guide to Thoreau's Maine,* edited by J. Parker Huber.

That night, under a crisp quarter moon, a loon calls. The sound is often described as demented but to me is the pure, unrestrained voice of the wild, repeated and answered from across the water.

I AWAKE TO THE CRACK of Garrett's ax against fresh spruce logs, rise to the smell of bacon in the big skillet, and dine on hash browns and eggs to the tune of Sofia's jokes. ("What do invisible cats drink? . . . Evaporated milk!") Soon I am leaning into my new north woods stroke, on the Penobscot River, watching weeds on the bottom sway like golden hair in the current. A family of mergansers swims noisily away; a belted kingfisher scolds. Every now and then, we dip our cups into the water to drink, a rare opportunity in America today, though one Thoreau would have taken for granted.

He traveled in 1853 with his cousin, George Thatcher, and an American Indian guide, Joe Aitteon, who provided ducks for their breakfast, to go with tea and hard bread; Aitteon spent most of his time trying to shoot a moose. When he succeeded, Thoreau carefully measured it. "I did not wish to be obliged to say merely that the moose was very large."

Our tribe has moose on the mind, too. We find tracks of *Alces alces Americana* in the mud adjacent to our next camping spot, upstream of Ragmuff Stream. The cloven hoof marks look huge. Like Thoreau, who wrote, "this hunting of moose merely for the satisfaction of killing him . . . is too much like going out by night to some wood-side pasture and shooting your neighbor's horses," we are not hunting moose. We want the simpler satisfaction of seeing one.

Thoreau stayed just up the hill from our next campsite, in Smith's Halfway House, named for Ansel Smith, who provided lodging for loggers and later moved a bit south, to the shore of Chesuncook Lake. The foundations of the old inn are still visible, as is the rock-lined well in the pasture taken over by bunchberry, wild pink roses, and red hawkweed. Fodder was grown here for draft horses used in the days when trees were cut and dumped into the rivers, where they stayed until the spring thaw carried them south.

"Thoreau could not have foreseen that so much of this would remain," Garrett says, showing us around.

However, clear-cutting has eliminated vast stretches of forest just beyond the tree-lined banks, and now there is little but cut-over country a few see-fars from the last drinkable river on the eastern seaboard. These lovely woods are little more than a screen for one of the great timber bonanzas of all time.

In Thoreau's day, logging and hunting were the reasons one traveled in the woods. He went against the grain when he wrote, "Every creature is better alive than dead, men and moose and pine-trees, and he who understands it aright will rather preserve its life than destroy it." That was close to heresy in the twilight of Manifest Destiny, when the building blocks for a young nation were still coming out of places like this. Looking at the remains of Smith's forgotten enterprise and considering the effect of massive clear-cuts beyond the river's fringe of trees, I believe that Thoreau's genius was not in taking off for the wilderness and making sense of the experience. His genius lay in having the imagination and daring to question prevailing attitudes about its use—questions considered antisocial and no doubt anti-American. Now we're at the end of the headlong exploitation of phenomenal resources that was already humming when Thoreau passed through.

By the time camp is set up, a certain easefulness prevails. Susanna and Sofia sit on the bank, painting with watercolors; Svea has Robyn stretched out on the ground, to "release tension" by passing her hands through the air above "bad energy fields." She asks Robyn, whose eyes are dutifully shut, what color she would like to see, and Robyn says, "Sky blue," which is the overarching hue in this remarkably dry, insect-free passage through country notorious for precipitation and bugs.

Supper is Cornish game hen, parboiled, split and roasted in the skillet, seasoned with paprika, garnished with sautéed chopped celery and almonds and served with rice and squash sprinkled with Parmesan cheese. Passing clouds briefly release raindrops that dimple the river but distract no one from dessert: pineapple upside-down cake that inspires Sofia to squeeze her fingers together in an Italianate gesture of pure perfection. This sort of camp life is a dying art in an age dominated by freeze-dried protein and carbs inhaled for biking up the next mountain. But real food leads to real contemplation in a sepia, stop-frame moment, and I imagine Henry David scribbling on his scraps of paper and Joe Aitteon inspecting his leaky bark canoe.

Before bed I open *The Wildest Country* and learn that the dying Thoreau's last words were "moose," and "Indians." In the middle of the night, I am awakened by the sound of something large stamping about in the shallows. I crawl out of my tent and find Robyn already about, wearing a headlamp. "*Moose!*" she whispers, having seen it clamber up the far bank.

THE RIVER SLOWS and broadens south of the Hay Islands. They were named for fodder grown there to feed the hearty Percherons that hauled logs in Thoreau's day and stayed on the islands year-round. Before we know it, we are on Chesuncook Lake, an Indian word meaning "a place where many streams emptied in." A bald eagle tilts high above this luminous, ever-expanding realm that pushes the far bank into the distance.

We are faced with two days of flat water, but first will spend a night on sheets, at Lake House, built on the site of Ansel Smith's structures in 1864. The original homestead included a blacksmith shop, an icehouse, a barn, and a log house that Thoreau considered "but a slight departure from the hollow tree." All this is gone now, the white clapboard house that replaced it owned by a young couple from Massachusetts, who decided to escape with their five children to a simpler era.

The landlord meets us on the shore, in trim beard and Bermudas, loads our gear into a trailer, and hauls it up to the broad front porch that overlooks the water and the mile-high thrust of Mount Katahdin, Maine's reigning peak. The village of Chesuncook is readily accessible only by boat. A dirt road crosses marshes that require serious all-terrain capability, and the landlord uses a World War II troop carrier to bring in their supplies.

Chesuncook has a dozen year-round residents. The Conovers lead our tribe to The Store in the Woods for a bottle of homemade root beer and then on to the village church. *Pilgrim's Hymnals* are scattered over the seats, to be picked up when the old pump organ begins to wheeze. Each Sunday, an itinerant preacher is brought in and put up at the inn. "He either preaches to a dozen people, or thirty," says Alexandra, "depending on whether or not they come over from the boy scout camp."

The cemetery, the ultimate New England social register, is populated with simple stone memorials, including those of Tommy Smart, Ansel Smith, and a sprinkling of Penobscot Indians—all of them associated in some way with Thoreau's memory. Mick Fahey is buried here, too, his gravestone inscribed with a verse from Alfred

Lord Tennyson: "I am a part of all / That I have met." Fahey died in 1985, and Garrett and Alexandra stand for a while over their old friend. She says, "We brought that stone here in a canoe."

The Lake House porch was made for sitting, and that we do, gazing across at Gero Island. Dinner is served in the dining room, under gas lights unavailable in Thoreau's era and quaint in ours.

ON OUR NEXT-TO-LAST day, we cover fourteen miles on flat water, the wind, usually a constant, banished along with the rain. Scattered across the bright surface of the lake like carefree children, we chatter among ourselves. Sofia reads a Harry Potter story; Alexandra, paddling alone along the shore, sings; Susanna paints ever-present water, gray, glacier-smoothed rocks on an endless beach, sere fallen timber like rough-hewn steps leading to the bright, birch-framed mysteries of the interior.

Thoreau wrote in *The Maine Woods*: "Not only for strength, but for beauty, the poet must, from time to time, travel the logger's path and the Indian's trail, to drink at some new and more bracing fountain . . . far in the recesses of wilderness." The same can be said for the rest of us. I have mastered a version of the north woods stroke (*mastery* is a tricky word in Maine), and everyone has shed some doubts about the necessity of modern conveniences. It's all a kind of playacting, of course—and beneficial because of it. If we can keep alive the once-vital connection between the physical world and us and have fun at the same time, then who can object?

We are comfortable in our new element, knowing, of course, that Garrett will get the fire going and Alexandra will bake something to celebrate with on our last night together—iced lemon cake, in fact, decorated with yellow loosestrife, red osier dogwood, and pearly everlasting, to be digested while watching feathery northern lights climb the vast Maine sky. So no one really cares when wind comes up in the afternoon. We can already see the island where we'll camp; we can almost smell the wood smoke.

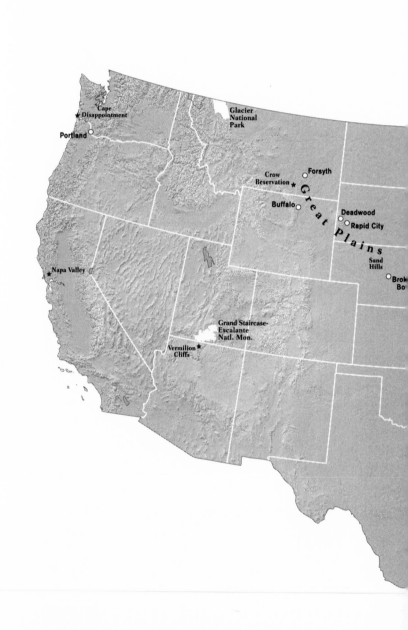

Cape
Disappointment ★

Portland ○

Glacier
National
Park

Forsyth ○

Crow
Reservation ★

Great Plains

Buffalo ○

Deadwood ○
○ Rapid City

Napa Valley ★

Sand
Hills

○ Brok
Bo

Grand Staircase-
Escalante
Natl. Mon.

Vermilion ★
Cliffs

III. GHOSTS

Chapter 13

OLD DOMINION

Don't come looking, because you won't find it. To begin with, the river will confuse you, rising as it does high on the eastern slope of Virginia's Blue Ridge and running for a time in afternoon shadow, before turning east, toward the Chesapeake Bay, and passing through country alternately pastoral and deeply forested. Stands of oak and softer woods are bound up with honeysuckle and wild rose that in spring overpower even the smell of fresh running water. The sycamores and tulip poplars close to the river draw on this inexhaustible source, their massive, gracefully contorted trunks younger than the distant fields but old enough to remember when this was another country altogether.

An ancient landscape by American standards, it was named for the Rappahanocks, who once populated the entire Atlantic seaboard. But Africans and Europeans have been here so long that they have infused the land with their presence. A visitor glimpses it in ruined rock walls, where woods have sprung up again, in cellar holes filled with the tumbled dreams of the diggers, in wheel ruts worn into the earth and abandoned when paved roads led the people off to lives unimaginable.

One such track leads here, and if you find it, you probably won't continue. It resembles an old farm road, half-swallowed by dense bottomland growth, the high sides testament to a century of hooves in harness and another century of rubber tires, beginning in one county and leading to another, emerging into light, where a little pie slice of open land stretches along the bank of the still-nascent river.

The house has a tin roof that has kept the lines sharp, clapboards, and a screened side porch. The view out front is of a field hayed twice a year by a farmer living elsewhere, the view out back of grass and scattered trees dwindling to a narrow vortex where shadows and river converge. This spot once served as a stage stop, or so the story goes, and since then as a refuge for yeoman farmers, including at least one black family, all unwitting strugglers after the Jeffersonian ideal first expressed not too many miles to the south. There's no hog wire left on the runty apple trees now, just the scars. The grass in which the house sits is mowed in season, if indifferently.

There is no other structure in sight, no sign of human existence in the westerly view but a power line, and in the impoverishment of winter, distant lights of settlement crowding the boundary of Shenandoah National Park. In summer, house and land are enfolded in the soft, vernal riot that is the Virginia piedmont.

What's left of the road, after it passes the house, is a track for white-tailed deer and the occasional bear down from the mountains to maraud in cornfields and in the more interesting morsels of our civilization. Penny and I bought the place despite the facts that the well water was cloudy, the river volatile, and the property demanding, and set about adapting to country life, if only episodically. We already had a home in Washington, and so fell into that problematical category: weekenders, city slickers, cocktail farmers whose acre and a half works its way into their lives as a foundling might, even as they work for it, painting, plumbing, digging, mowing, sawing, hauling, and tackling other jobs both unanticipated and ignominious. Much has been written about the restorative power of houses and their surrounds, and it is mostly true.

FOR A TIME, I was the only person I knew who traveled with a pair of hip waders in the trunk of his car, not for pursuing brook trout on the east slope of the Blue Ridge but for getting to the house in those times of what Virginians call falling weather. Our low water bridge wasn't much of one when it was raining, and none at all in the episodic monsoons that rolled over the mountains, when our little river rose like some liquid behemoth, transforming the landscape and making anybody on the wrong side of it extremely thoughtful.

At such times, there was too much water over the bridge for a car, but the river could sometimes be waded. Then it attested to its designation as wild and scenic. In good weather, we rarely discussed the river. In falling weather, it bobbed in our conversation; with more rain, passage across the bridge became dicey, and the subject close to unavoidable. Wading a little river is a merry pastime in the furnace of summer, runoff lapping at your bare ankles, but at midnight in leaf-drop time, amid encapsulating woods and drenched fields, wearing cold rubber boots, you feel there in the darkness a powerful, enveloping force urging you to drop your duffel and grocery bag and travel, upended, toward the Chesapeake. Dimpled by downpour in early light, festooned with limbs and small trees, the river was at other times an ugly mutant trying to climb the stone wall, streaking across the lawn where no river should be, jamming flotsam behind the lurching hickory trees.

In summer we slept with the bedroom door open onto a small deck, within earshot of the river, separated from the bug-laden night by screens. Except in the hottest, driest times, the river eked out an existence in defiance of the elements, insinuating coolness and constancy. It didn't murmur, contrary to popular opinion, but offered subliminal suggestions, a Rorschach for the ear: distant cheering, snow in the sycamore boughs, wind. These alternate and blend in a damp continuum beyond which lies the shadowy stuff of dreams.

One warm night, I woke up to an unaccustomed sound and padded to the open French doors in the bedroom.

The lawn lay deserted in moonlight; the woods were one massive backdrop. I looked down and saw, three feet away, separated from me by a screen, a large black bear eating mushroom mulch out of the flower crock. I would later blame the river for conspiring with another wild thing to defraud us of petunias, and sleep, but for the moment, I was in sphincter control. My shout sent this intruder off the deck like a two-hundred-pound rocket-borne licorice gumdrop.

There are 3.5 million river miles in America and some ten thousand rivers over 25 miles long. They vary in size from the Mississippi and the Columbia at their outpouring maws to little guys like this one, but then they all have to start somewhere. Ours starts here, more or less. It flows on to absorb the Rapidan and other fine whitewater in these parts, dropping toward the coastal plain, part of the watery web that in the mind's eye holds the United States together. The health and vitality of the hinterland can be measured by what runs in our rivers, which too often includes agricultural and industrial waste.

The Rappahannock's protean ability to expand in flood time, even this close to the headwaters, forced us to purchase flood insurance to get a mortgage. Rivers are considered useless if they can't support boating, meat fishing, and swimming. We settled in summer for occasional immersion, and suspended a hammock over it and dipped in our feet while reading in the shade of the swamp maple. Also wrested up limestone for building a wall to contain a raised garden. Riverine biology is undidactic: A great blue heron in August descends like a collapsing card table to prey on minnows and frogs, a

OLD DOMINION

185

pair of wood ducks furrows the surface in an October dawn and explodes into the wind, the mink with the blond tail swims downstream in November. Deer use the river as a sight lane. I have heard the clatter of their hooves on the river stones in winter, when ice and death are in the air, glad that I was on the right side of that Stygian equation.

That same watery strand binds us to the earth and to our origins; it, too, depends upon nourishment from above, an act of faith even if the godhead is gravity and the pilgrim one little river.

EVEN SMALL COUNTRY holdings can use a pickup truck; that was the argument, anyway. I had never owned but had long wanted one, for reasons unclear, not the modern, sculpted mobile lounges that resemble giant suppositories as much as trucks but a midcentury presence with unrepentant edges, aero-defying bulk, and a breath redolent of hot oil. A 1954 Ford would do nicely, I had thought when I read about it in the *Valley Trader,* an offering of last-ditch commodities for the variously needy ("Dirty telephone, $5. Good for shed use").

It sat in a cinder-block garage on the outskirts of Winchester, Virginia, Patsy Cline's birthplace, an old steel warrior in a latter-day sarcophagus, very red, the matte finish bespeaking the attentions of some shade-tree mechanic doing after-hours junker restoration. That the job was less than professional added to the luster: no mint conditioning here, no high gloss, chrome fetishes, or furry dice, just a hauler in the gloaming of its existence.

The owner had bought the pickup already restored for

his son, he told me, who had found it incompatible with dating. "It don't leak," the father added, and opened the door to reveal a black shag interior and, on the dash, a starter button like a silver nipple.

I got in and pushed it, turning over unseen a fundament of American power and élan, fed by a carburetor, itself a treasure of tubular brass for mixing and dispersing vital fluids: worlds within worlds, all outsourced through a "short stack," a tailpipe that terminated directly beneath me and that breathed sonorous hydrocarbons. Driving around the block, I saw the son's dilemma: This was a two-handed machine. *Caveat emptor,* intoned the ghost of Henry Ford. Old trucks are protracted cardiac arrests; pickup CPR is learned in shop class, and my conversance with the internal combustion engine was limited. I bought it anyway.

Driving the thirty miles south to our place, listening to the throaty rhythm of six firing cylinders, I tried to remember 1954 and would later come up with a tabulation of that year: Elvis recorded "Heartbreak Hotel," and the Supreme Court handed down its *Brown v. Board of Education* decision, legally ending segregation. Our soldiers were home from Korea, and Americans were still talking about the Kinsey Report. President Eisenhower was driving to golf outings in a white Eldorado; the House Un-American Activities Committee was chasing so-called subversives among the Presbyterian clergy; I was thirteen, in Memphis, home of the world's largest Baptist church.

Later, on my back in the grass, I gazed up at a firmament of crud-encrusted steel: bowed springs, antiquarian driveshaft, transmission cracked in a mishap occurring between the invention of the cure for polio and the death of John Lennon and patched with a kind of metallic peanut butter. This solution would require, I learned, cornmeal in the transmission oil to further plug the leak. (Polenta, I discovered, worked best.) This assemblage passed for advanced technology in 1954, yet oblations performed upon it were simple and satisfying. No megabytes hidden in this beast, no binary math or electronic fluting in microscopic silicon bowels, just explosion and venting.

The truck lived in the shed with the washing machine. Away from home, it introduced me to people I would not otherwise have met, like the bearded figure wearing an old backpack and standing at the edge of the highway. "I knew an old Ford wouldn't pass me by," he said, climbing aboard. "I had one once, just like this. Threw a rod."

His name was Luke Moonstone, and he had clearly been on the rougher rides of the 1960s. Christ had saved him, he said, although he was no evangelical aggressor. "You don't read the Bible," was all he said on the subject, "it reads you." I let him out near the library, where he wanted to check out a biography of Robert E. Lee but felt guilty diverting time from the Bible. "Maybe it'll be checked out," he said hopefully.

The older man in the John Deere cap said at the gas pump, "Nice truck," a common observation. "Now that's when Ford built *trucks*." America's industrial icons had succumbed to history's soft determinism, and in his comment lived this and every other affront since 1954: Elvis and Ella on television, Volkswagens, the

Kennedys, busing, pot, the Tet offensive, Watergate, Betty Friedan, catalytic converters, Hondas, the recognition of secondhand smoke, 2 percent milk, and, of course, Bill Clinton.

The pickup's serious duty was traveling to the dump. This county shrine, known drolly as "the Mall," brought together domestic detritus for enlightened recirculation. Every Saturday, pickups sat in the shade of sycamores waiting for other pickups to offload the avowedly broken or soiled that would be taken up again by those more tolerant of imperfection. The regulars unlimbered poles with hooks attached for plucking out the odd saucepans, car seat, or clock radio. Old clothes draped the Dumpster: overextended stretch pants and jumpers of vibrant print, but also a tired Harris tweed jacket and a fleece-lined suede coat.

Larger items—rusty stoves, old kitchen cabinets, punctured wading pools, dinette tables—were set aside and often barely touched dirt before being levitated and borne away. The scramble was for choice items that would not qualify as such in an urban setting; there was no bickering, however, no unseemly rush for the cordless hair dryer or the smashed gun case, just a resolute shuffle, a speculative prod. You kick it, you own it. Meanwhile, the sheriff sat in his cruiser in a secluded farm lane across the highway, awaiting weekenders lacking a dump sticker and surreptitiously divesting themselves of wine bottles and old newspapers. The sheriff's writing of a five-hundred-dollar ticket was a treasured spectator event.

I found a chrome lamp requiring only a new switch

and two monumental rough-cut planks that I made into a bench next to our well house. My best gift to recycling was a satellite dish I jerked out of the ground in a fit of aestheticism, knowing that I had a vehicle capable of carrying it away. This was deemed unwise, "a damned shame," as a regular put it, meaning I had given up contact with the outside world. I left the dish anyway and drove on into Flint Hill for milk and a newspaper, and when I passed by again, the satellite dish was gone.

The Mall's gone now, graded over, and a new dump opened elsewhere in the county. The new place allows only minimal trade and is watched over by a stern public servant. Bottles and newspapers are sorted, and no building materials allowed. People are in a hurry, with little conversation. My truck is gone, too, I must confess, to make room for other things in the shed and to alleviate the constant care an old vehicle requires. But it made me happy, with a kind of liberating speed not set by law but by mechanical tolerance. My prelapsarian progress through the county was a source of consternation to some, the unarticulated past riding in the bed behind me, an indecipherable accumulation of life that I could never unload and was still trying to get comfortable with, as I was with the reflection in the old rearview mirror.

THERE WERE NO pickups, restored or otherwise, parked outside the mansion where the hunt breakfast was held. It didn't start until well after 1 P.M., and I knew not to expect grits and eggs, but oysters and clams on the half shell, served in the foyer. This was followed by beef

Wellington and Bloody Marys consumed in a large room notable for the porcelain, the depth of pile, and theme throw pillows—a fox's face in needlepoint, the words "Hold hard." Everything was bracketed by oils of horsemen at a gallop, the painted scenes remarkably like the real one out in the back of the fieldstone mansion.

Beyond lay rolling meadows of piedmont Virginia marshaled by fences and woody verges that accentuated the breadth of grassland, and spotted hounds of distinct lineage, white-tipped tails held high. The animals belonged to the Orange County Hunt, and with them were a handful of riders in black coats and high riding boots, whips in gloved hands resting on the pommels. The riders looked remarkably like the people eating and drinking except that the indoor versions had replaced their black coats with houndstooth check and removed their spurs; some had gone home and put on entirely different outfits. "We had half an hour of tone after the first fox went to ground," said a woman with her hair twisted into a bun, a bit of dirt on her jodhpurs.

"Tone" was provided by the hounds—never "dogs." Hounds didn't bark or bay, but "gave tongue." Before giving tongue, they drew through coverts so as to open on a fox. The object of the hunt was not to catch the fox but to almost catch him for a while and then to run him into a hole, where he was usually left. Cold, wet days were best for the scent of the sleek, reluctant quarry.

Virginia's horsiest senator rode slowly up the meadow on a black stallion; the man's pretty, lightly lacquered companion sat astride a bay. Neither seemed particularly interested in tone. The governor-elect of another state was already in the house—he owned it—having hung up his silk hat; he surveyed the sitting room as if it were a swale between "whippers-in" (members of the hunt staff who kept the hounds together). The master of the hunt had replaced his "pink"—a classic red coat not to be confused with Nantucket's reds—with plaid over a vest of canary yellow. The local contingent of Du Ponts had brought houseguests; draped about the room were adipose, middle-aged preppies and one emaciated scion, but mostly the crowd looked healthy.

Jacqueline Onassis used to ride with these people. The former First Lady was no "hill-topper"; she didn't sit back or "coffee-house," but pushed the equestrian envelope. Fox hunting has its dangers. One of the senator's former wives, Elizabeth Taylor, injured her back hunting here and ended up in the hospital. "Oh, there are wrecks," said a pleasant English woman. "You know, groundhog holes. Falling over backwards while going up creek banks. I got stuck in the fork of an oak after being thrown, my feet dangling. Would have gone straight through if I was less well-endowed."

Fox hunting was indirectly responsible for much of the view, having forestalled development in a region famous for it, and was worth it for that alone. Hunting created an extended, private concourse through which a capital ganglion of wealth and influence tallyhoed most weekends, giving nearby Middleburg a reputation as "the ground-zero of American fox hunting." The town's streets were shingled with derivatives: the Hunt Scene, the Finicky Filly, Dominion Saddlery, the Fox Room, the Iron Jockey, the Thoroughbred. Police cruisers had foxes painted on the doors; the exclusive local girls' school, Foxcroft, divided classes into teams of Foxes and Hounds, and students could board their own horses.

To belong to the Orange County Hunt, one had also to own land within its boundaries. This hunt was arguably the most exclusive in America and had a curious history, being located not in Orange County, New York, where it originated, but here in Fauquier County, Virginia. In 1905, E. H. Harriman, master of the hunt, fed up with the hard winters in New York, moved it officially to Virginia. He bought land and traveled down in his private railway coach; other New Yorkers followed. More property was acquired and farmers were cajoled into letting the newcomers ride through.

Outsiders rarely get a view of these workings, just the occasional spectacle of horses over panels on a weekend, and the distant cry of the hunting horn. At most Orange County weekend hunts, a foreign emissary was in evidence, the guest of a member responding to a specific request or smoothing the way for some foreign jaunt of his or her own. The senator, however, was not known for advancing any notion more ambitious than courtship. "He used to insist on a white horse," said a fellow rider. "He charged around, acting like an ass, but lately, he's calmed down."

So, never pass through coverts when hacking to a meet, or fail to say good morning to the master. Do not get ahead of the master. Do not take your own line, do not shout when you view (never "see") a fox but stand in the stirrups and point with your hat, never your finger. Never stand in the way of others if your horse refuses a jump, never hover over a person who has been thrown, and never ever fail to say good-bye to the master at the end of the day.

The county has other hunts as well, as do nearby counties. Collectively, they still act as a valuable preserver of open space, although that is changing, as is the cast of riders. Newcomers are as often as not more interested in investment and development than holding hard; prime turf is being lost to other interlopers yearly, and squabbles over boundaries increase with the median price of real estate.

AN ENTIRELY DIFFERENT sort of hunting is represented in the mountains far west of Middleburg. I am eating a moose steak and listening to a hammered dulcimer played in a nearby tent, under a harvest moon wreathed by smoke from hundreds of campfires. The cook, Char (her "rendezvous" name), offers more potatoes from the iron pot, her deerskin fringe swinging in the glow of candle lanterns. Her husband, Buzzard, strikes sparks with flint and steel to ignite a cotton wick used to light his cigar. Bear props his hand-sewn boots on the wooden chest, and Lizard begins yet another story about shooting long rifles.

The two hundred year after-burn of the American Revolution has reached into the present, to a gorgeous spot in the Allegheny Mountains that used to be Virginian and are now West Virginian. I can imagine this scene taking place in 1800, despite the chemical toilets, and feel the allure of a natural setting free of the disembodied voices of the twenty-first-century America,

including cell phones. My fellow campers are all members of the Widowmakers, a club of competitive long-
rifle shooters who could have been mountain pioneers
sharing a meal and a smoke. Even their nicknames derive
from kinship with the past. "Char" is an abbreviation of
Frozen Charlotte, a type of porcelain doll popular in
colonial America; in her other life she's a notary public.
Buzzard, a computer consultant, helps municipalities
program their traffic lights. Bear manages the agricultural enterprises of an eastern university, and Lizard
claims no profession.

The men, heavily bearded, wear handspun shirts
and deerskin leggings they made themselves. *Buck-
skinning,* the collective term for this replication of the
ways of the earlier age, involves an interest in history
and a certain nostalgia for a simpler America, but also
a desire to leave, even if temporarily, a culture they see
as lacking in individuality and craftsmanship. Lizard's
story about the "old" days of rendezvousing in the western United States—the 1970s—is funny and profane,
resonating with exploits like the filling of cannon with
horse manure for blasting the tents of rivals in the all-
important shooting matches. Those raucous times, too,
are gone.

Arrayed on racks in front of our tents are the graceful
silhouettes of contemporary long rifles. Bear picks his
up and wipes away the dew with a cloth. The rifle was
made by a contemporary master in New Hampshire,
but in the firelight is indistinguishable from an implement emerging from colonial Pennsylvania or Virginia.
Risking sentimentality, he says, "This is a work of art,"

and gets no argument from me. So are the handmade tomahawks and beaded belts that convey a poignant yearning for another time. I wonder if someday Americans will gather around a reconstituted computer in an urban wasteland and replay ancient video games. This is more than playacting and less than the rigor exemplified by the Conovers of Maine, but keenly felt, anyway, and a testament to the power of the past.

In *Notes on Virginia,* Thomas Jefferson wrote of the Blue Ridge visible from Monticello, and the Alleghenies just to the west of it, as the last barriers to westward expansion. Beyond them, he believed, lay answers to mysteries both scientific and cultural. Reading him in his time, one would have gotten the impression that the Mississippi River lay just out there, not hundreds of miles away, and that beyond it stretched country inexhaustible by any civilization then imaginable.

Chapter 14

BUFFALO COMMONS

AT THE END OF THE EIGHTEENTH CENTURY, ALL trade west of the Alleghenies passed through New Orleans, which was then in French hands. The Louisiana Purchase in 1803, arguably Jefferson's greatest accomplishment as president, proved a powerful geographical determinant in the development of the American character, one that he recognized early on. He seems to have envisioned this inner kingdom, extending north and west from the Gulf of Mexico into what is now Canada, as a kind of preserve that would sustain his yeomanry and somehow keep these landowners and the nation whole. Comprising 500 million acres bought at three cents each, even today the purchase makes up almost a quarter of the United States, and most of it lies within what became known as the Great Plains.

Probably no region, with the possible exception of the American South, has engendered more confusion and cliché than the Plains. Alternately referred to as a desert and a national breadbasket, an endless expanse of nothingness and a soulful land of unique beauty, a savior of the dispossessed and a creator of the same, the Plains is in fact a distinct geographical entity within a dozen modern states, running from the Texas Panhandle to Saskatchewan, all of it beginning at the 98th meridian, beyond which rainfall is too scarce for large-scale agriculture and sometimes for any at all.

Within its boundaries lies a highly varied social landscape, its long-standing and acute economic travails bound up in drought, distance, federal subsidies, and myth. Included in that landscape is the American bison—buffalo—lately cited as a possible communal redeemer and cattle substitute. I went out to see for myself if the Plains were really different and to test, among other things, the viability of buffalo steaks in a universe of beef.

SOMEWHERE AROUND Broken Bow in central Nebraska, the Great Plains officially begins. The Sand Hills rise like ancient dunes rolling toward an unseen ocean, what's left of spring green gashed with white sandy blowouts and old cattle trails bordered by stalky yucca. Evergreens struggle in the windbreaks, and cottonwoods draw on what's left of the Ogallala Aquifer, all of it serenaded by hopelessly optimistic meadowlarks riding deviant fence posts.

Each soft ridgeline promises a longer view of some defining geology, but each reveals the same prospect: grass running to the edge of blue-gray sky, and tufts of cloud radiating out from some weather front too distant to seem relevant. Abandoned farmsteads rise and fall regularly, the solution to this problem not anywhere in evidence. The possibility that any one activity could end the much-heralded decline of rural life here seems increasingly unlikely if you are actually traveling the Plains, yet two decades ago, a pair of academics in distant, crowded New Jersey claimed just that. Their proposal—a combination of herding, ecotourism, and benign neglect—was audacious and visionary, its vehicle the quite palpable American bison.

They were Frank and Deborah Popper, their original idea the now-famous Buffalo Commons that, if ever realized, wrote Anne Matthews in her excellent book, *Where the Buffalo Roam,* "would become the world's largest natural and historic preservation project, a massive act of ecological restoration that boldly reverses three centuries of American settlement and land use history. Visitors to such a commons would see the heart of the continent as Lewis and Clark first knew it." The Poppers' research, she added, "suggests that the epic struggle to tame the Plains, and to mine it of topsoil and oil and gas and water, has . . . been the largest, longest-running environmental miscalculation in the nation's history."

So the once nearly extinct, wild, and intractable buffalo became not just a theoretical component that made this couple somewhat famous but something more: a loaded metaphor capable of inspiring Americans who knew nothing of the Plains, and enraging those who lived here. If buffalo best embodied the Plains' natural and historical essence, buffalo also symbolized the threats of isolation and savagery to Manifest Destiny. The Buffalo Commons quickly became a code phrase for the redemption of an aspect of the romantic past and the harm of meddling outsiders who wanted to impose "government"—meaning outside—controls on such a large piece of the United States that contains only 3 percent of the population.

Near Johnstown, Nebraska, the ground has been plowed and, sure enough, is blowing away in a kind of living dust bowl diorama. The erosion stops abruptly when the grass starts growing again, an elemental bit of instruction. "A prairie excels at survival," Matthews also wrote. "Prairie-grass seedlings spend their energy growing roots . . . that can reach six to ten feet below the topsoil. . . . Pioneers said the prairie literally rang, or twanged, when the plows turned over its dense underlayer—'a storm of wild music,' one wheat-farmer's child recalled, many decades later."

SIXTEEN MILES NORTH of Johnstown stands a rustic sign put up by The Nature Conservancy for its Niobrara Valley Preserve: short-stemmed lavender penstemon on the roadside and along the river walnut, hackberry, burr oak, and, a bit higher, ponderosa pine. Beyond the little visitors center, in deep shade next to a year-round spring, is a house that was built in 1901 from a kit that arrived by rail and buckboard. The manager, John, emerges smiling: salt-and-pepper mustache, a pair of firefighting boots, a round of Copenhagen in the snap pocket of his shirt, and, in his past, a Ph.D. in ecology with emphasis on handling fire in open prairie.

"We have six ecosystems here," he explains, after introductions, and ticks some off: mixed grass, deciduous, boreal, prairie. Twelve miles of river frontage on the north side of the Niobrara, about half of it with bought-out development rights, and twenty-seven miles on the south side, which is mostly rented out as pasture. Here flourish buffalo in two herds of several hundred head each and derived mostly from stock imported from Montana in 1999; cows are culled at twelve years of age, slaughtered in nearby Valentine, and sold as organic meat to longtime customers. John and neighbors hired for the purpose round up the animals once a year for brucellosis vaccinations, a political move to forestall complaints by other ranchers, and to dust them with pesticide for parasites; otherwise, the buffalo are left to themselves, even in winters, when they sweep away snow with their impressive heads to get at the grass beneath.

We go looking for buffalo in his pickup, gathering speed to get up steep sand ruts. Trucks are used for roundup, not horses, "because horses give out after the initial round. A buffalo can run all day. We tried ATVs, but they didn't impress the buffalo. They'll fight them." I scan the horizon and the wooded folds for a glimpse of these audacious beasts. There are lots of hiding places in this landscape where freestanding pines and other trees are becoming more numerous every year because prairie fires have been eliminated. The illusive buffalo is to remain so today.

John, a libertarian, blames spreading woody growth for the diminishment of the natural grasses, but a bigger culprit in the decline of the Great Plains is federal farm subsidies for unsuitable agriculture in arid regions. "You can grow twice as much wheat and corn in Illinois without irrigation than you can here with it. Why spend all that money and deplete the water?"

That was the Poppers' argument, but John is no fan of the couple's ideas. Back in the 1980s, the Poppers pointed out that almost all of Nebraska's fifty-two counties were losing population, a trend reflected elsewhere in the Plains, but John claims the Poppers overestimated the emigration "that has mostly stopped. Cattle ranching is sustainable here," he adds, "and it's not subsidized. Sand Hills ranchers have figured out how to do it." This explains the rarity of buffalo elsewhere in the neighborhood twenty years later: "Why switch to another species that's more difficult to manage than cows?"

Heavy construction of the corral and "squeeze tub" used to hold buffalo for inoculation indicates how intractable and dangerous they can be. "You get in there during roundup, and you're a dead man. These are still wild animals." They're also just one element in the Conservancy's effort here to reclaim land and instill some basic ideas of conservation in a beautiful, remote piece of the puzzle of isolation. John adds a phrase that will stick with me: "This place has existence value even if it doesn't bring back buffalo, even if no one ever sees it."

THE COUNTRY SLIPS by, the miles shorter than they are elsewhere. Fingers rise from steering wheels of pickups in the universal Western greeting, the hand coming off the wheel on occasion. The town of Valentine has hearts painted on the sidewalk, a bank's facade bears an old brick fresco of a longhorn drive, a stark reminder of what cattle once meant to these parts. The Pepperbox Lounge offers various cuts of beef—sirloin is the specialty—but no mention of buffalo. Another source of tourist revenue for the town is the lovely Niobrara River, which runs through a wildlife preserve, its bluffs shaded by ponderosa pines and paper birches in the seeps whose moisture maintains all the riparian growth in an arid land: wild grape, little bluestem grass, and deciduous trees alive with flycatchers and red-winged blackbirds.

Between Valentine and Merriman, little farmhouses have black holes for windows, though the rooflines still run sharp and straight. The double-wide or prefab box next door is the new abode into which the family has moved, but there are no swings or children. Lonely windmills suck at the aquifer almost as an afterthought; more than one abandoned grain elevator announces an approaching settlement. Cody, Nebraska—A TOWN TOO TOUGH TO DIE according to the sign on the outskirts— seems without citizens, but there are pickups parked outside the Husker Hub Bar and Grill. The paint-peeling facades of stores without merchandise face a well-maintained park shaded by locusts, and further up the street stands a derelict clapboard house, an ancient tractor pensive in the bluestem and the sun-blasted door without a handle. But nearby stand houses with well-tended flowers and, more convincing than the town's motto, kids' bicycles dumped on well-watered lawns.

The Sand Hills peter out just west of Merriman, where Ted Turner's vast land holdings begin. I leave the highway, cross Burlington Northern's tracks, and take a dirt road. A house on the edge of a square mile of lush meadow is shaded by old elms; several knocks on the door bring an elderly man in Levi's and a plaid shirt, polite but wary. Yes, he says, Turner's his neighbor and he has no problem with him. When Turner's buffalo get out, men come on ATVs and drive them back. Turner did limit access to his land to someone wanting to get to a gas-drilling pad: "He's being a butthead about that." This rancher has no interest in buffalo as a commodity; he has sold most of his cattle and gets 3,500 bales of hay off a thousand naturally watered acres and sells it.

His wife's calling him to Sunday dinner for two. I thank him, and he says, "You betcha."

Cattle grates mark a succession of frontiers, an occasional mailbox the only clue to human habitation. Turner owns some millions of acres in the Plains and intends to make money on buffalo—and canned hunts on some of his many ranches—although his spokespersons in Atlanta and Bozeman, Montana, have little to say on either subject. The question is, Does Turner run buffalo to profit through "vertigration" of an exotic product, raising, slaughtering, and selling the meat directly to the consumer through his own burger franchise, Ted's

Montana Grill? Or does he do it to protect endangered species and habitats that can only be done on this scale by people like him or the federal government? Or does he simply want to make people shake their heads, and say, "There goes Ted again, doing something unexpected." The answer is probably all three. Still, he has injected into Western land a useful example that boosts local biomes.

Finally, I see some buffalo, on the far side of barbed wire. I get out of the car; they watch me approach, and begin to run, en masse and not far, turning and running back again, eddying upon themselves as animals in a herd will do. Heavy in the shoulders and shaggy, they have a deceptively determined gait and an obvious curiosity. Dust hangs over them in a nimbus of western light, what's left of their wildness accommodated to fences and roads and reinforced cattle chutes.

Down the road, the ranch owned by Turner—one of many—must have once been a bustling outpost. But few hands are required in this new sort of wrangling, and ATVs don't need feeding and currying. A young man in a T-shirt and seed cap with a tightly rolled bill emerges from the house, friendly if also wary. He's the foreman and he met Turner, he says, on another Turner spread to the south, took him fishing, and is now in charge of an isolated fiefdom like some faithful Roman general sent to Gaul. He's not much interested in what happens to the product once it's out of his sight, when the buffalo are fattened up elsewhere on grass before slaughter. There are few overlapping needs between buffalo and other ranches, and "partnering" with neighbors is tinged with class issues going back to the absentee landlords of the late 1800s, when European grandees bought big spreads and eventually ran most of them into the ground.

You could say the West really begins at Chadron, near Nebraska's western edge, where a Wal-Mart has turned its back on the broad views of buttes. No alcohol is served on Sunday; many cars have license plates from elsewhere, this being on the tourist trail to the Black Hills, the Badlands, and various "visitables"—Mount Rushmore; Fort Robinson, where Crazy Horse was murdered by soldiers; the Oglala National Grasslands to the north.

The next morning, I cross the grasslands, passing more deserted houses. Pronghorn antelope and their newborn stamp exotic silhouettes on the horizon, and whimbrels nest in the sweet clover, abnormally warm weather seeming to have disrupted their migrating habits. In Ardmore, South Dakota, yards are full of weeds and collapsing roofs, but the most striking aspect of this ghost town is the abundance of cars and trucks, some going back to the 1940s. They are parked everywhere, paint transformed by the sun into strange, vivid colors, interiors gutted and headlights dangling like defenestrated eyeballs, the abandoned workhorses of a once sustainable community. I can't help but wonder if the town still has existence value. Sixteen citizens lived here as recently as 1980; Ardmore was visited by President Calvin Coolidge in 1927 and survived the Depression without one family on welfare. Now, across from the deserted general store, a sign ironically proclaims: BEEF — IT'S WHAT'S FOR DINNER. Today, there's no one here to eat it.

A tilt-up, unfinished casino marks the boundary of the Pine Ridge Reservation twenty-five miles on, amid big dry expanses of plowed land without cover crops and with little prefabs and double-wides set in difficult terrain. Intense small ranching lies all around. The "hand-feed buffalo tour" is an option, although these Lakota Sioux are the only tribe in South Dakota without a herd of their own. The most common signs warn against speeding, with big Xs and the words "Marks the spot" and "Why die?" A battered sedan is on my tail, crazed windshield apparently the victim of a baseball bat, driver and passenger obscured by the cracks; they pass on a blind curve, across a double yellow line, the car shaking, and beat me into town.

Pine Ridge is hot, the main street under construction and the detour rough, with more cracked windshields and stoic faces. Parked outside the Higher Ground Café is a pickup with a shamanistic piece of bone wired to the grill; inside the café, I'm served a cappuccino by a lovely woman and her accommodating, bored teenage daughter. I sit on the deck, watching big, drifting turtleback cumulus.

Wounded Knee lies just to the northeast, where a faded sign at the edge of the highway explains that here the last armed conflict between the Sioux and the U.S. Army occurred in 1890. Minneconjou and Hunkapapa men, women, and children were mowed down with Hotchkiss guns and butchered in retreat, after protesting reduced beef rations for the reservation and indulging in ghost dancing that the Indians believed would bring back the exterminated buffalo and also protect them from bullets. A tour bus pulls in and blocks the view of this history lesson, and I drive up the hill to a sad visitors center.

Inside, the inevitable dream-catchers are for sale, and Homeland Security T-shirts with a picture of a mounted warrior. The woman at the desk was only three years old in 1973, when two federal agents were killed nearby in a latter-day protest of federal hegemony; she remembers her father resisting the feds "and the half-breeds who teamed up with them." Now she sells beadwork and refers visitors to a communal volume of Edward Curtis's famous photographs of declining Indian nations.

THE PRAIRIE EDGE emporium in downtown Rapid City offers various Indian tchochkes—painted drums, buffalo headdresses—and there are buffalo sausages rolled in pancakes in Talley's. But no buffalo roams the meat lockers in Albertsons supermarket or any menu I can find, including that of the historic Alex Johnson Hotel, with its two stuffed buffalo heads over the big stone fireplace and more American Indian regalia for sale next to the ATM machine. Outside on the pavement are shoals of luggage and motor coaches disgorging tourists.

There is buffalo steak available, I discover, in a fancy Italian restaurant around the corner. I down it with a glass of Oregon pinot noir. The meat could be a cross between beef and venison, more flavorful than the former, more textural than the latter, altogether delicious.

Buffalo meat won't marble, as the marketers discovered when they first tried to engorge the animals with corn in feedlots and found that this practice produced only a layer of fat under the skin, a kind of cellulite underwear. Grass is what bison require and what gives the meat both flavor and value, along with an absence of injected hormones and antibiotics.

Back at the hotel, I bypass the crowd at the elevators and climb eight floors to my room. Looking out over the city, I remember poor old Ardmore and its legion of abandoned vehicles. What were once chariots of delivery have become toxic pods dumped in a now ambiguous landscape. It seems that the number one enterprise in Rapid City, as in so many other parts of the West, is not cattle or any other traditional Western commodity, but cars: selling, servicing, fueling, and catering to them and those inside. This obsession is something overlooked by the Poppers, that and the ever-increasing press of travelers who are less interested in ecotourism than packaged visions of human enterprise since the conquest. Gasoline and related products have brought as many problems to the Plains and other Western states as solutions; energy exploration, mining, and other development pose a greater threat to agriculture and enduring community than had all the buffalo herds of yore, even if they could be brought back by ghost dancing.

THE INTERTRIBAL BISON Cooperative occupies a prefab building on the outskirts of the city. The director, Mike Fox, comes from the Fort Belknap Indian Reservation in Montana and wears a baseball cap from a saddler in Cody, Wyoming, indications of the commonality of this vast country. He's proud of an assemblage of fifty-seven tribes from nineteen states, with a collective buffalo herd of fifteen thousand. He also proudly explains that the successful lobbying of Congress has brought a million dollars in grants to various tribes. Buffalo, he says, have contributed their bit to health and profits, but more importantly "have made a difference to our culture. People see more and more buffalo coming back and start researching customs and rituals lost over the last hundred years. There has been a spiritual revitalization— sun dances, powwows, memorial giveaways. Songs associated with the buffalo hunt are recovered from neighboring tribes, even in Canada. It all kind of came out of the woodwork."

As for the economics, tribes use the meat or sell it on the hoof. The money goes into tribal programs, like Head Start and those for heart disease and diabetes, "one of the biggest problems. We want to get back to our original diet before reservations and government rations devastated the Indian people. Buffalo are more efficient to raise, more economically viable, and better for our health."

Collectively in the Plains states, American Indians have 10 million acres that could be buffalo range. "Once you step outside the regional population hubs," he says, "it's back to the big open." Much land on the reservations is leased to white ranchers, but only the American Indian population has grown in the big open, a source of consternation to some whites. "We've got a return of the people and the buffalo at the same time," says Fox, and he laughs. "Sounds kind of crazy."

BEYOND SIGNS FOR Wonderland Cave, Trout Haven ("1.5 million caught"), and Sugar Shack Burgers lies Deadwood, South Dakota, the supposed inspiration for the profane television show. Here, too, black, horned heads preside over public spaces—little casino bars where tourists mix with locals dressed for killing, six-shooters strapped to their hips. These citizens of Deadwood have assumed the personas of famous and not-so-famous psychopaths, their weapons loaded with blanks for reenacting 1870s gunfights scheduled every few hours. In the Coffee Saloon (aka café), Turkey Creek Jack Johnson is drinking what looks suspiciously like a latte. He wears a fringed leather jacket along with his pistol, and has a real beard and a tattooed earlobe. "Wild Bill wasn't around here for long," he informs me, without prompting, "but I survived."

The photos on the walls are of abandoned houses and fields that recall the Depression. The artist's statement interjects some reality into this setting: "The simple, unpretentious world of the 1930s has disappeared, and what has replaced it is frightening."

IN SPEARFISH, South Dakota, hideous McMansions crowd Interstate 90, which spans northern Wyoming. By now I know that the big open is made up not only of prairie and plain but also of forests, mountains, verdant river valleys, badlands, and suburbs. Not all of this can be seen from blacktop roads, even less from a superhighway; only gravel leads into the heart of the matter, lots and lots of gravel: gray, red, and white, dusty, slick as soap when it rains, devoid of directional signs. If you don't know where you are, you don't belong: the cowboy tautology. But Westerners generally bestow more generosity on clueless strangers than would ten Bostonians, New Yorkers, or Washingtonians.

I'm bound for Sheridan, Wyoming, in the shadow of snow-topped Big Horn Mountains, but pull off on impulse at Buffalo, Wyoming. Beyond the usual welter of chain motels is a charming little main street with a diner—the waitress's button says, "Yes, I'm having a good day, and, no, I'm not married to the cook"—a sporting goods store, and a historic hotel, the Occidental, with period furniture in the lobby and a saloon with the original dark-paneled bar from the 1880s. It is associated in some vague way with Buffalo Bill Cody, as are many bars in the northern Great Plains; Cody was for a time the most famous man in the world, thanks to the international venue of his wild west show, which I suppose makes the buffalo as famous. These walls are hung with every horned head imaginable, including both American and Cape buffalo.

The attached Virginian restaurant is named for Zane Grey, who supposedly peopled his purple prose with characters he met here; the menu proudly proclaims Prairie Bison Rib Eye, Buffalo Top Sirloin, and Bison Medallions Occidental over Fettuccini, all from "young animals that run the canyon rims and drink from pure mountain creeks."

This vision is tempered somewhat by the discovery that the town isn't named for the West's signature beast but for Buffalo, New York, home of one of the men

GHOSTS

who tossed names into a hat at the town's founding in 1877. Ranchers around here have been supplanted by retirees, tourists, and energy developers; fine food, graphite fly rods, and upscale motorcycle paraphernalia are as much "traditional" products now as cows. History itself is a commodity. The local historical museum is as spiffy as any enterprise in town and has a well-stocked gift shop to match its exhaustive collection of American Indian and early settler artifacts, ready for any stripe of visitor.

Oil, gas, and coal seem to dominate the northern plains, despite the tenacity of the cowboy image; carbon extraction has become the equivalent of the Poppers' subsidized, incompatible agriculture, this and the ever-expanding federal highway system. Near Decker, just over the Montana line, soft bituminous has been scraped from the earth for a generation with gargantuan draglines that have radically altered this arid, fragile landscape. I want to view one at its work, but the guard in a shack that sits in a wasteland of mining spoil just shakes his head.

The Tongue River meanders through beautiful dry country with pink burns high in the hills above sparse juniper and sage flats that run down to emerald banks of fast-moving water. Roads in this dry country raise storms of dust; ranches are isolated, the sky a particular powdery blue. Occasional bleached logs evince long-collapsed homesteads, rusted bedsprings strewn in the alien blond grass (brome) particularly poignant. I have been to this part of the northern plains before, thirty-odd years ago, to write about the effects of strip mining and the attempts of local ranchers to forestall it. The big coal companies were then exercising eminent domain to get at the coal, a holdover from the days when the railroads were granted subterranean mineral rights by legislators in far-off Washington, D.C. Now, some of those same ranchers are battling methane gas development, which threatens to swallow their beautiful Tongue River.

THE CROW INDIAN Reservation happens to surround the Little Bighorn Battlefield National Monument. At the Intertribal Bison Cooperative in Rapid City, I make arrangements to talk to Rides Horse, who is reportedly in charge of the reservation's large, loosely managed buffalo herd. Little do I know that I am to be thoroughly vetted once I get to the reservation. Tribal headquarters, a yellow brick building with plywood on some windows, is quite lively inside, people coming and going between offices. A woman with a sheaf of papers directs me to the rangy, bespectacled Rides Horse, who listens dutifully to some questions about the herd and says, "Let's go talk to the wrangler."

He leads me down the corridor, past a message board with posted warnings about methamphetamine and cattle repossessors, and out onto a landing where three men in Levi's and cowboy hats are talking. I am introduced to one man, who immediately hands me over to "the man in charge." Trimming his fingernails, the man in charge listens until the trimming's done, then says, "Come with me."

He leads me back down the hall and into a side corridor, opens a door into a room with a long table at which sit a dozen men, and leaves me. I'm struck by the men's stature, heft, and seriousness; the one at the end of the table— middle-aged, in a fresh plaid snap-pocket shirt—looks me over without expression, and waves me to a chair.

His name's Alvin, and *he's* in charge. The herd, he says, numbers about 2,500 and pastures in a remote corner of the reservation that's 7,500 feet above sea level and snowbound in winter. "We just busted through," he says, of the wranglers who ride up over a 10,000-foot pass every two weeks to camp and check on the herd and watch for heli-poachers. The roundup's next month—July—for vaccinating and some culling. About 130 buffalo are killed each year, mostly for tribal members who have appealed to the chief, and sometimes for white hunters who pay $2,500 to track and shoot a bull. "It gets pretty Western up there," he says. "Years ago, Clint Eastwood called and said he'd give the tribe fifty thousand dollars to shoot one, and another fifty thousand as soon as it hit the ground. But there was a change of tribal administration, and it didn't happen."

No ATVs or pickups can maneuver on that high range, just horses; it takes three to pack out one dressed buffalo, so the process is both demanding and historically correct. Alvin spent every summer there until he was twenty-six, with his grandfather and his father. "In those days, each of six tribal districts would decide how many buffalo were needed, and who would shoot, skin, and butcher. We'd all go up in a caravan and when we came down again, there'd be a giveaway." He pauses. "The average Crow thinks buffalo are a good thing. We never get tired of looking at them."

How satisfying it is to envision buffalo as restorative not just of landscape, but also of tradition. The tribe's minister of culture has some caveats about that, however. I meet with him later in his office, amid an impressive array of papers. "Only a couple dozen tribes retain their culture and language," he says, Levi's tucked into the tops of his cowboy boots and a green feather in his hatband. He has a master's degree in linguistics from the Massachusetts Institute of Technology, but that's another story. "We are one of those tribes, but even though we profess to the spiritual customs, we're ninety-seven percent Christian." That same percentage of the reservation is leased to whites, mostly for ranching, but buffalo remain a potent cultural force.

"We lost contact with them in the eighteen-seventies, when they were wiped out. It was the beginning of the end of our way of life: Buffalo had nourished, sheltered, and clothed us." In the 1930s, the federal government provided some new bison to the tribe, but that herd was killed off, too, he says, by the U.S. Park Service in the 1960s to make way for Yellowtail Dam. Since then the herd has gradually been built up again, but "we've lost many of our belief ways and discarded our sacred bundles." Although the sun dance—like the ghost dance—was outlawed by the feds in the late nineteenth century, the Crow continued, until 1908, singing songs that went back to the mid-sixteenth century.

"Some still carry on our ways. Some try to blend them with Christian ways. We"—the handful of true adherents to Indian culture—"call them the chicken shits. Others are outspoken in defense of the old ways, but don't really understand them. Meanwhile, the tribe regresses, losing minerals, and land. We're down to about a million acres from almost forty million from the treaty of eighteen-fifty-one. We're faced with extinction."

There are about eleven thousand surviving Crow, more than half of them living on the reservation. "We have diabetes, cancer, heart problems, because of the diet and loss of nomadic ways. We're the richest indigenous nation on paper, but in reality, we live in poverty. There's seventy percent unemployment, and three and four families under one roof, so you don't see the homeless. Our teachers are certified to teach white, middle-class Anglo-Saxon children. Most Crow aren't English speakers, and language is the key"—not only to success in America, but also to survival. Without bitterness, he adds, "We know the problem and solutions, but not how to implement them."

I drive forty miles further into the reservation and, following directions, hike up a knoll overlooking in the far, far distance emerald plateaus high above the Bighorn River. There the buffalo roam; although I can't see any, even with binoculars, I can conjure up what must be the happiest herd east of Yellowstone.

GRAINY DUSK IN Forsyth, Montana, a collection of services for agriculture and mining, and some ailing historic buildings just off the interstate. I leave a nicotine-redolent motel filled with engineers and mechanics working on the big coal-fired power plant down at Colstrip and walk across the railroad tracks to the friendliest looking of several saloons. Four cowboys are drinking

Bud Light and clearly enjoying themselves: short, solid guys with big hands and big belts, two in big hats. I order a beer, get up the nerve, and ask one if he's a rancher; this silly question is treated with respect. Yes, he ranches forty miles away, and no, he has no buffalo. Does he know anyone in the neighborhood who does? Well now, he says, thinking, and puts the question to the others; soon they're pulling names out of the cigarette smoke. Most of the operators they mention are in buffalo as a hobby, but then the bar owner says, "Glenda Reynolds," and they all nod.

Glenda's famous, it seems, for hiring women wranglers and for other edgy behavior. "She'll draw on you if you push her," says one of the big hats. "She's up north of here, in the emptiest country you've ever seen."

After supper, I Google Glenda on my laptop and get the 7W Ranch in Sand Springs and a telephone number. I dial it, and a raspy recorded female voice declares the basics. I leave my number, assuming I'll never hear from her, but at 4 A.M., the phone wakes me up. "I'm on my way to the eye doctor in Miles City," she says, after my groggy introduction. "I'm leaving the pickup at Bud's Auto to get it worked on. Meet me there at ten o'clock."

HER TRUCK'S UP on the rack when I arrive, a shovel and other tools strapped to the back of the cab and dried mud all over everything. A loaner pulls up, and out of it steps a diminutive figure in big hat, sunglasses, snap-pockets, big belt, and worn black boots with upturned toes. She ambles over to confer with a respectful mechanic who towers over her, then she turns and gives me a hand rough as horn. I have offered to buy her lunch, but observe that it's a bit early for that, and Glenda says, "Not if you've been up since three thirty."

Eating a BLT in a chain restaurant, sunglasses off to reveal very blue eyes, she talks buffalo: "If they charge you, you ride uphill because they're about half lazy." If that doesn't work, "you shoot them in the nose with a thirty-eight revolver loaded with number nine bird shot." That treatment is usually reserved for "the snakes"—chronically uncooperative buffalo that she eventually kills "or they'll ruin the young ones" and butchers, cooks, and eats.

Her herd is down to about two hundred buffalo, on sixty thousand acres near the Missouri Breaks, so many miles from a paved road there's no point in counting. Glenda's been dealing with buffalo for eighteen years, as well as cows, "but buffalo are about three times as smart as Herefords. No two look alike. They can jump a fence, but they're too damn lazy" and so go right through if they feel like it. "That's why most ranchers hate them: Ranchers are hardheaded, and buffalo're hard to handle."

She's without a husband now, sixty-five years old, weighs maybe ninety pounds, has arthritis and multiple plates in one forearm shattered by a frantic horse she was treating for mountain lion attack, manages in addition to buffalo and cows a line of thoroughbred horses strong enough to keep up with the snakes, and raises her own vegetables. She spends her money on little but cigarettes, beer, and books, and over the years has taken in foster children and taught them to deal with life on a ranch without television or town. One of them, a younger woman, works for her now and is no doubt the origin of the Amazonian myth in places like Forsyth. In addition, her grandchildren are sent to her periodically for home schooling or "to get straightened out."

Ranchers' biggest problems, she says, are outsiders' ignorance, "and coyotes." I bring up the Poppers' vision of a buffalo commons, and she says without rancor, "That's bullshit. It would put cattlemen out of business. This land will sustain cows, and people have to eat. The land's not depopulated, but most people are old, like me, hanging on. Young people can't go out and buy a ranch, because everything's so high now."

I want to visit 7W, but couldn't get in with my little sedan. And Glenda has itinerant hands coming to help move cows, anyway. So I follow her to a jump-off point over some fifty miles of gravel roads on which her mud-caked, reconstituted pickup travels at seventy miles an hour and more than once leaves me alone in very big country. The sight of a distant white dust devil is the only evidence of Glenda, who is steering with one hand. After more than an hour of this, I find her parked on a high spot, with the Breaks barely visible to the north, across a vast depression full of ridges and valleys utterly unlike the country I have just traveled. It's green and empty except for a distant barn roof on the ranch where she grew up without cars or electricity.

Glenda lights a cigarette. "I'm about twenty miles out there, down in a hole, just shy of the Missouri," and there's something in the way this remarkable woman says it that suggests both pride, and longing. Clouds are piled above the chlorophyll-tinted universe that is Montana in early June; a curtain of rain is drawn across more miles of sky, with strings of moisture called virgas dipping and then evaporating before they touch the earth. But there's plenty of room for blue sky, too.

Chapter 15

GLACIER

I FIRST SAW GLACIER NATIONAL PARK ON THE EVE of an expedition to photograph grizzlies in the mid-1980s, when my focus was mostly upon impending death. The second time was to attend a conference more than a decade later, when I found my perception altered by the prospect of a "cultural," rather than a "natural," experience. What had earlier seemed threatening had become only interesting; what had been awesome, merely beautiful.

Glacier hadn't changed, but my relationship to it had. I asked myself if these two experiences could be reconciled at the passing of the century that had seen the national parks' creation in its early years. Was wilderness still the primary value, and civilization in the form of roads, lodges, and other emoluments of human visitation an intrusion, or had nature and artifice achieved a more equal claim on the imagination?

The view of the Rockies in east Glacier, across Swiftcurrent Lake, still embodies the awesome aspect of nature dear to Victorians. Massive Grinnell Point sits in the forefront of consciousness, diminished by the upthrust of the Continental Divide and falling away past barren headlands to the soft grays and greens of limestone and conifer. The curiously named Many Glacier Hotel is an aging tourist destination with a colorful provenance on the lake shore, a paean to the early marriage of commerce and sublimity that is by now an integral part of the scene: rambling gables, balconies with jigsaw patterns, chalet-style windows with busy moldings, broad-hipped roofs that throw deep shadows, all under generic brown paint that was peeling—a hyperthyroid European hostelry in pentimento.

A National Historic Landmark, Many Glacier Hotel was just one of many extraordinary structures built in the West to lure Americans to what was then a novel idea—national parks—among them Old Faithful Lodge in Yellowstone and El Tovar Hotel in the Grand Canyon. Many Glacier was the only one with this view of dwindling ice and alpine uplift, in a million-acre park billed as the American Alps. The slogan was not the government's but that of a railroad promoter and tourist visionary, Louis W. Hill, president of the Great Northern Railway and the park's unofficial impresario when it was established in 1910. He had taken his cue from the

Northern Pacific, which built the Old Faithful Lodge for rail passengers. Hill's Great Northern owned the land adjacent to the new park, and its president became Glacier's first concessionaire.

The Glacier Park Hotel Company served as the source of the park's first visitors. It was a grand business scheme to put well-heeled Americans in Pullman cars in Minneapolis, Chicago, and New York and ship them toward the setting sun. To receive them, Great Northern built hotels as impressive as Yellowstone's, but with a Swiss theme—Glacier Park and Many Glacier hotels and numerous mountain "chalets"—and kept the profits in an early example of a practice that would become increasingly controversial: leasing access to legally sanctioned wilderness.

Those early rail pilgrims to the shrines of Manifest Destiny stepped down onto the siding at East Glacier and into a view that included mountains in the background and an array of Blackfeet tepees set up in front of Glacier Park Hotel for dramatic effect. For the trip to Many Glacier Hotel, some boarded motor carriages: low-slung, rakish, with roll-back canvas tops, lovely on the open road and still in operation. At Many Glacier Hotel, guests were catered to by tailors, hairdressers, bellboys in lederhosen, and waitresses in flowered dirndls, or kimonos for the tea service under Japanese lanterns. Old photographs show women in long gowns and men in ties sitting on splendid new balconies, squinting under a high-country sun.

THINGS HAD CHANGED. Many Glacier Hotel was now a pastiche of Rube Goldberg Rustic, with cracks in the rubble masonry, sagging cantilevered roofs, rotten beams, homely steel trusses supporting balconies that in winter filled up with snow, and a cable and pulley arrangement rigged to support a bowed wall. A picture window broken by a rutting mountain sheep who mistook his reflection for a rival had yet to be replaced, while inside, in a corridor known as Stagger Alley, whole sections of wall leaned in different directions. A college student who worked here during the summers said, "I look at the floor when I walk by so I won't get seasick."

Upstairs, in a towering lobby with columns of local Douglas fir holding up four levels of balconies, Doric capitals, roof beams, and trusses all conspired in the forceful treetop geometry of the sky-lighted atrium, an effect augmented by an open fireplace with a towering copper hood. The old spiral staircase had been removed, a souvenir shop set up, and a makeshift portico tacked onto the front entrance to shelter the busloads of tourists.

Structures like Many Glacier are sometimes criticized for being elitist when they are not criticized for intruding upon wilderness. Part of the emotional freight is historical, the association of high society in raccoon coats with their latter-day counterparts in sweats by Ralph Lauren, even though the rates here and at other national park hotels were pegged to comparable upscale ones outside. Parks all over are now "improved" with railings, toilets, and bus service, with the claim that this is somehow democratic, the weakness of the argument evidenced all over the West in the glut of houseboats bobbing on dammed rivers, in paved highways altering high, wild valleys for the convenience of Winnebagos, and in demands by concessionaires for more construction in the parks.

Many Glacier Hotel said a lot about America before two world wars, when the country, like its parks, seemed inviolate. European references were needed then for authentication, whereas today a reference to Glacier as the American Alps seems no more apt than calling Switzerland the Montana of Europe. The hotel's exterior provided a didactic lesson in the need for national self-respect even as the setting demonstrated the restorative power of landscape. The lobbies of Many Glacier and the other hotels embody remnants of the American ideal, dispelling our emotional dependence upon the Old World and replacing it with a more inspirational component: a rough-hewn, indigenous vitality to match the spectacle of the forever possible beyond tall, westering windows.

Not long after Louis Hill stepped down as president of Great Northern, the company lost interest in its tourist endeavors. The rail line had been established; the hotels were expensive to maintain, the government not always compliant. Stephen Mather, the National Park Service's first director, dynamited a sawmill in 1925 after the railroad declined to demolish it, stating emphatically, "We don't have sawmills in national parks!" Ten years later, a Great Northern executive described the railroad's structures in the viewshed of its American Alps: "We must rid ourselves of these parasites."

The concession changed hands several times and came to rest eventually in Glacier Park, Inc., which asked for millions of dollars from the government to fix up Many Glacier. The two-hundred-odd rooms are all rented these days, but before, the place lacked amenities like private bathrooms, and the staff provided earplugs to mute rattling hot-water pipes at night.

A cluster of small cabins down the road, built in the 1930s in "tepee circles," recalled the Depression, when the balm of nature was considered crucial. Glacier Park, Inc., and the National Park Service brass wanted to tear them down and replace them with modern units renting for much more. "What we're talking about is re-development," I was told by Glacier's superintendent, a big, amiable Park Service veteran in shiny black cowboy boots. Like his counterparts throughout the system, he had considerable latitude in such decisions and conducted himself more like a padrone in a hacienda than a government employee. "The corporation's got possessor interest," meaning investment over the years.

Multiply Glacier's opportunities by the six-hundred-odd concessionaires within the national system. Yet the Park Service's mission is "to conserve the scenery and the natural and historic objects and the wildlife . . . to provide for the enjoyment of the same in such manner and by such means as will leave them unimpaired for the enjoyment of future generations."

Rooted in the creation of Yellowstone in 1872, and in the Forest Reserve clause of 1891 and the Antiquities Act of 1906, which allowed presidents to set aside public lands from development, the parks became official with the National Park Service Organic Act of 1916. That year, Many Glacier Hotel was completed, two years after Mather was brought in by Woodrow Wilson's secretary of the interior to deal with the nation's already peerless collection of landscape: Yosemite, Sequoia, Mount Rainier, Crater Lake, Mesa Verde, Grand Canyon, Zion, Glacier, Rocky Mountain. The "borax king" who had made a fortune in cleaning powder, Mather determinedly opened up and managed the new park system with grudging support from Congress, and today the number of people going to national parks every year exceeds the population of the United States.

"WE HAVE A SALEABLE product. The Park Service can't endorse, but there are lines of products out there we could associate ourselves with."

The speaker, the Park Service's associate director of cultural affairs, is an envoy from the Potomac to a group of intermountain superintendents, planners, and resource specialists gathered in the Moccasin Room. There are lots of snaps on pockets, and a few clasp knives in leather holsters. The theme of the conference is the preservation of historic structures, and the associate director is talking money, specifically, Barbie dolls. "They could be licensed to use the Park Service uniform, and we could get six percent of the millions Barbie dolls earn every week. The Park Service is a career that young girls can aspire to, so it seems to me that we could do worse than rake in the dollars."

There are other ways, she adds: solicitation, bond sales, frequent-flier mile swaps, clubs like Ducks Unlimited and Trout Unlimited, and the big one, corporate sponsorship. Target stores donated $5 million to the restoration of the Washington Monument. The miniature Washington Monuments set up in Target parking lots were "a big hit. We have names of companies that want to be associated with us."

The assistant director of Yellowstone National Park takes the podium to also advocate corporate sponsorship. Use wooden signs, he suggests, not neon, and "bring in guys who're heads of corporations and you put them on horses. They ride like sacks of potatoes—it's an ugly thing to see—and then you put them in a cabin up in the mountains. By the next day, they're hooked, and pretty soon they're opening their wallets."

Such "principled flexibility" strikes some old-line rangers as huckstering. The proposal to dress Barbie dolls in ranger uniforms finally brings the superintendent of Capulin Volcano National Monument in New Mexico out of her chair. "Do we really want a big-chested, anorexic girl with small feet to be the image that future park rangers aspire to?" she asks. "As I understand it, Barbies are engineered so they can't even stand on their own two feet. The Park Service is low-key and should remain that way: Do our mission, preserve the resource."

IN THE FINAL YEARS of the nineteenth century, the park system was seen primarily as a Western phenomenon. Despite the 1926 addition of Shenandoah, Great Smoky Mountain, and Mammoth Cave national parks, the park system remained an agency, in the public mind, limited to the preservation and promotion of grand natural landscapes.

Horace Albright, the man who succeeded Mather as park director, wanted to expand the agency. In 1929, he convinced Congress to create several historic parks in the East. The War Department possessed a variety of memorials, forts, and battlefields, and in 1933, riding in the backseat of a car with Franklin Roosevelt on a trip from the Shenandoah to the capital, Albright spoke feelingly of the advisability of transferring all the War Department's historical properties to the Park Service. Roosevelt complied.

The Historic Sites Act of 1935 designated the National Park Service as the federal agency responsible for historic preservation, enunciating "a national policy to preserve for public use historic sites, buildings and objects of national significance for the inspiration and benefit of the people of the United States." In 1960, secretaries of the interior were empowered to designate national historical landmarks. Secretary Stewart Udall endorsed a management policy that recognized three different categories within the Park Service—natural, historic, and recreational. The most important single stroke by Congress, the National Historic Preservation Act of 1966, authorized the Park Service to keep a National Register of Historic Places, which lists sites of local significance as well as national landmarks, public and private.

The temporal span is three thousand years, from prehistoric Arctic and Southwest stone assemblies to the polished marble of the Franklin D. Roosevelt Memorial, the cultural diversity daunting, as is the diversity of materials. Some eight thousand structures are of military significance, from early Spanish fortifications to a Nike missile site at Golden Gate National Park. There are Park Service wooden hulls afloat in San Francisco harbor, and a destroyer in Boston.

Also falling under Park Service jurisdiction are railway cars, bridges, and 1,300 roads of historic interest, an overarching cultural web from which the service cannot escape. Glacier National Park, one of its stars, gets about $11 million a year, Yellowstone about $17 million. A superstar like the Presidio gets $19 million. Competition among natural, cultural, legal, and developmental cohorts is part of the problem. Park superintendents insist upon autonomy, and congressional pork-barrel politics funnels money directly to them, with every superintendent having his or her own contacts. The Park Service became a popular subject with the new "conservatives" in Congress who saw it as a source of income for supporters, and as a way of attacking big government by depriving the service of the money it needs to function efficiently and then pointing out the bureaucracy's foreordained failings.

The parks produce an estimated $10 billion a year for those on their peripheries. Members of Congress demand parks in their districts, regardless of the qualifications, and exploit existing parks to produce local revenue and votes, in violation of the Park Service's mandate and the system's integrity. Some eight hundred thousand people pay to fly over the Grand Canyon every year, for instance, at great profit and to the detriment of the experience for those on the ground. A six-lane highway was proposed to narrowly pass by Petroglyph National Monument in New Mexico and to be used by twenty-four thousand vehicles a day.

In the case of Glacier National Park, there is loss of more symbolic value: the glaciers. They have been diminished by two-thirds since 1850, as a result of rising global temperatures. Average temperatures in the park have risen almost two degrees Fahrenheit since 1900, and scientists predict that the Grinnell Glacier and others for which the park was named will disappear entirely before 2040. Any visitor hiking on or near the glaciers today is struck by the preponderance of flowing water and flawed ice.

Added to these baleful facts are others relating to water quality and environmental degradation. Water quality is bound to suffer massively from methane gas development just across the Canadian border. Moreover, under the feet and tires of two million annual visitors, all of them eager to experience an American version of the sublime even as it dwindles before their eyes, the general health of the park will no doubt deteriorate.

MY LAST NIGHT in the park was spent in Lake McDonald Lodge. The hotel was built by John Lewis, a speculator who reportedly won the land and buildings in a poker game. But my thoughts stayed on the questions raised at the conference. With visitation at record levels and the country prosperous, why were we now saddled with Parks Unlimited, CEOs on horseback, and the possibility of a Barbie doll in a green uniform and hat? It seemed a short step to the Taco Liberty Bell, Disney's Old Faithful Hot Water Slide, El Capitan by Kodak, and the Boeing-Wright Brothers Museum.

Lake McDonald Lodge is a cameo version of Many Glacier: imitation flagstones incised with slogans in Blackfoot, Chippewa, and Cree, rough-hewn posts and railings, furniture with bark, cedar columns, and support beams. Chinese-style lanterns covered with hieroglyphics of vague prehistoric mien hang above Indian print sofas, but the overall effect is that of the European alpine hideaway serviced by a bellboy in lederhosen and retrofitted with electronic keys.

It seemed to me, under the gaze of stuffed heads— mule deer, mountain sheep, pronghorn antelope, even a caribou, all shot by old John Lewis—that the Park Service stood not just for the preservation of parks and historic structures but also for a certain old-fashioned ethic. The notion of the incorruptible Park Service ranger was of inestimable value, an asset that no other federal agency possessed and one our politicized corrupt, "conservative" Interior Department now seems determined to undermine. What those at the conference talked about wasn't so much preservation as integrity and standards that are the last redoubt of American innocence, which today is threatened in its entirety.

I still hadn't reconciled the nature-versus-culture problem, and then I remembered a dream in the Apgar Range, within view of this lake, ten years before. Then, I went to sleep scared and hungry in a tent near a populous grizzly highway and dreamed not of bears but of riding a train through a blighted urban landscape. This night, between clean sheets and within the jig-sawn fantasies of a dead railroad tycoon, I dreamed of pure rushing water and the daunting immensity of trees and stone.

Chapter 16

ESCALANTE

THE VERMILION CLIFFS ARE A SPECTACULAR geological continuum extending all the way from the Grand Canyon in northern Arizona into the Escalante country of southern Utah. Imagine a vast arc of flaming rock with the Colorado River at one end and Bryce Canyon at the other, the cliffs' deep crimsons and magentas running along miles of eternally stressed sandstone.

The cliffs can be seen from U.S. Highway Alternate 89, which takes the low road from Page, Arizona, to Kanab, Utah, the latter town once the southern hub of the Mormons' land of Deseret. This landscape lies within the Arizona Strip, its distant plateaus bearing old Piute names—Shivwit, Uinkaret, Kaibab. Wind and water shaped them, the broad valleys silver-green with sagebrush and juniper, and the high forested tablelands of confusing, sometimes frightening aspect.

Atop the Vermilion Cliffs sits the Paria Plateau, named for the ancient occupiers of this back pocket of the West. They have been gone from this landscape for roughly a thousand years, and we know them because of what they and other Native Americans left behind. Collectively, these artifacts and ghostly remains of dwellings serve as a palimpsest of ancient civilizations, if only you have eyes to see them.

Peter W. Bungart, an archeologist, does. He explains that the Ancient Puebloans, once referred to as Anasazi ("ancient enemies" in Navajo), arrived about 300 B.C. and introduced agriculture. "They made pottery because they were growing squash, corn, and beans, which required pots."

He's standing on a sloping shoulder of the plateau, still under the Vermilion Cliffs. In shorts and brimmed canvas hat, a pack on his back containing lunch (bread and avocados), topo maps, a battery-run Global Positioning System device, and other tools of the itinerant student of the long gone, he looks like a day hiker. All around us, in red sand under the blue sky, lie some of the pottery shards as well as knapped flint and smooth stones used as tools—debris that has been cast in the millions by the elements and by various peoples across thousands of square miles.

Bungart could pick any one of them and tell you its

provenance. Much of this reliquary, however, lies in the midst of impromptu tracks of all-terrain vehicles. He's employed by the Wilderness Society to inventory this part of the vast, arid Southwest so rich in artifacts that it has drawn thousands of archeologists to the hottest research turf on earth. The Paria Plateau and Vermilion Cliffs form part of the relatively young National Landscape Conservation System, some forty-six million federal acres in large, scattered parcels in the West, kept intact not as national parks but as spectacular public space.

The NLCS—the bureaucracy's uninspired name for a heroic vision—was established back in 2000 by President Clinton's secretary of the interior, Bruce Babbitt, to provide extra protection for whole landscapes. But most Americans have still never heard of it. The system's sheer size and complexity—more than two hundred parcels from New Mexico's Kasha-Katuwe Tent Rocks to Oregon's Cascade-Siskiyou Range, from the Upper Missouri River Breaks to California's Carrizo Plain—defy easy description. In short, the NLCS embodies, in the West, the last and best of old-time America.

Locked within its gorgeous, commodious confines are answers to some of the country's most intriguing cultural and scientific mysteries. One way to assure their continued protection is to compile lists of the prehistoric structures and objects beneath the surface of what could liberally be construed as an American Mesopotamia.

We walk on through a scatter of painted pottery shards, then plain, ridged ones from broken cooking utensils. Decades of grazing, prospecting for oil and gas, and recreation have wiped out large settlements of departed natives. But by chance we find ourselves standing next to an abandoned house site, the tumbled, mostly buried stones faintly outlining the shape of rooms lived in before the Renaissance. The subtlety of the site adds to its poignancy. This would also attract those who steal artifacts from public lands, either for sale or for a private collection, far from the gaze of officialdom. "Pot hunting's a way of life around here," Bungart says. "The BLM needs to close some roads because that would discourage misbehavior and theft."

The appointed administrators of the Bureau of Land Management, however, have no interest in doing so. In fact, they are opposed to protection, on political grounds. A lesser satrapy within the Interior Department, the BLM is responsible for 260 million federal acres. Created in 1946 by combining the General Land Office with the Grazing Service, the BLM is devoted in theory to multiple use of these lands but in fact tilts heavily toward development. The agency claims to lack sufficient funds to properly police areas like the Paria Plateau, "but they lack the will, too. They're always working on management plans, and meanwhile the resources are trashed."

On the way back to the highway, we stop to watch condors, successfully relocated from California, soaring above the Vermilion Cliffs. This is just one instance of nature's prevailing with the help of science, on land that belongs to everyone. Another advantage is protected backcountry that doesn't require heavy backpacks, as some wilderness does, and has not been compromised by pavement or posted lectures on geology, history, and dubious "sponsorship" that always come with a price. Here is land historically resonant that can be experienced much as it was a century ago, with few people and regulations, and much still to be discovered.

THE NATIONAL LANDSCAPE Conservation System has narrowly survived because nowadays "locking up" Western resources on public land is frowned upon by privatizers both inside and outside the present government, denounced by Western politicians, and nibbled at by lobbyists and industry functionaries appointed to fill crucial slots within the Interior Department and who then exploit public property in their own and their allies' interests. Of the units included in the NLCS—fifteen national monuments, thirteen national conservation areas, thirty-eight wild and scenic rivers, 175 wilderness and wilderness study areas, more than five thousand miles of national historic and scenic trails, a forest reserve in northern California, and a mountain in southern Oregon—most remain imperiled despite their official status. Many of these landscapes are threatened not just by developers and their congressional enablers but also by careless, sloppy visitors, cowboys *manqué* on all-terrain vehicles, and latter-day desperados who bear shovels and ravage the land and steal not only cacti, rocks, and arrowheads, but also human skeletons.

This is just one such problem facing Utah's 1.7 million-acre Grand Staircase-Escalante National Monument, which abuts the Vermilion Cliffs. Grand Staircase-Escalante, to the north, was named for the rising cliffs and plateaus and for the Escalante River that has carved up much of the landscape. The area has some four thousand recorded archaeological and historical sites, most of them eligible for the National Register. But these amount to only an estimated 3 percent of the monument's total number of sites. Culturally, they span ten centuries and include a smorgasbord of treasures, from lithic to can scatters, from petroglyphs to old corrals. And most of Grande Staircase-Escalante is unsupervised and therefore unprotected.

Administered out of Kanab, the monument has been resisted locally since its inception. Its workers have been ostracized in town; one monument worker who wore his uniform to the supermarket was advised that he might be shot. "The primary fear," he told me, "is that citizens are being shut out by the federal government. My barber is one of fifteen kids, and they made a living cutting cedar posts on the monument. They're afraid they're losing some of their heritage, and their sense of ownership."

The fact is, they never owned it or the cedar posts. Utahans, like residents of other Western states with significant public lands, petitioned the federal government in the mid–nineteenth century for inclusion in the United States, formally accepting the reality of public ownership of much of their surrounds. Since the federal government was to give each state enough public land to support its school systems, a bargain eagerly entered into by Westerners, their claims of ownership—or "rights" as they are viewed by revisionists of history—are ridiculous. The claims represent a small group's attempt to take land illegally from the rest of the nation, and during the second Bush presidency, these local scofflaws have been not just enabled, but encouraged.

Kanab, a Mormon town of about thirty-five hundred, is the seat of Kane County and the threshold of much off-road driving on public lands. Most evenings, outside the Mexican restaurant on the main drag, all-terrain vehicles can be seen sitting on trailers attached to pick-ups, everything covered with a patina of mud and dirt. Kanab and Kane County have a reputation for resisting federal mandates, particularly those limiting access to public lands and conduct upon them, with all-terrain vehicles providing a persistent, destructive means of political expression.

In November 2005, Kane and neighboring Garfield County officials went to court challenging BLM's re-source management plan in an attempt to get part own-ership of the hundreds of miles of federal roads and trails in the monument. There, trespassers had already torn down two dozen signs that restricted vehicle use. The violators set up more than two hundred of their own signs inviting off-roaders to drive wherever they pleased; not only were the trespassers not prosecuted, but the BLM decided to leave the signs standing.

Contacted by telephone and asked why, the BLM's acting director in Utah says, after a long pause, "It goes back to a question of valid rights. There are different approaches to different problems, and various options, administrative and legal." He won't say the signs are legal, but neither will he say they are illegal. If the counties get control of the roads and trails, it will open the monument to official anarchy, disrupting wildlife, threatening untold archeological sites, and radically altering the character—and the experience—of the land. The Wilderness Society, the Sierra Club, the Southern Utah Wilderness Alliance, and the National Trust for Historic Preservation have joined the suit on the BLM's side because "we thought it a bogus suit," says the attorney for the Trust, "and thought the BLM might try to settle too leniently."

Rewarding the county would set a disastrous precedent, although backdoor settlements are a common maneuver for transferring public property to private ownership. The acting state director halfheartedly denies that any such settlement is BLM strategy: "We're looking to resolve this in a way that meets federal standards and respects both interests." But the fact that the county's unlawful actions are encouraged by the agency says worlds about the way public lands are viewed at the Interior Department.

I ask the monument's manager, a thirty-two-year veteran of the BLM, why people aren't arrested when they break the law on federal land. Caught between the requirements of stewardship and the demands of local and national politics, he declares that the roads and signs dispute is "a Utah issue" and acknowledges that people often ask him why Utah isn't subject to the same federal laws as the rest of the nation.

LESS PUBLICIZED but no less unlawful incursions onto NLCS lands are common in other Western states. The situation is exacerbated by oil and gas exploration, rural sprawl, and grazing. In the southwest part of the Arizona

Strip, near the Colorado River, is the remote Grand Canyon-Parashant, a national monument with sites dating from ten thousand years ago to the late 1800s. There's no official presence there to discourage defilers of archaeological sites, which include Piute camps with metal and glass artifacts from their early contact with the U.S. Army and white settlers, and fences that keep out trespassers are repeatedly torn down.

The ranks of motorized joy riders in Aqua Fria National Monument are fed exponentially by the citizens of nearby Phoenix; the monument contains more than four hundred recorded sites, among them multi-roomed pueblos and complete, interrelated Native communities (the Perry Mesa Tradition) dating from 1250 to 1450 A.D., which could provide crucial archaeological pieces to the Southwest's prehistoric puzzle.

Pot hunters persist in the Canyons of the Ancients National Monument in southwestern Colorado, which probably contains the nation's largest concentration of cultural artifacts. Close to Mesa Verde National Park—a protected, somewhat homogenized, very different experience for visitors—Canyons of the Ancients protectors can recite the same litany of pot smashing and grave robbing. Defacement and destruction of signs put up by the BLM continue, despite the fact that the place attracts thousands of hikers, mountain bikers, and horseback riders annually.

Further afield, in Wyoming, what's left of the Mormon Trail, an entity in the NLCS, suffers similar abuse, in addition to a typical increase in mineral exploration, for which inspections are notoriously lax everywhere.

Industry and development impose upon Pompey's Pillar in Montana, on the Lewis and Clark Trail, and in the Cascade-Siskiyou Range near the Oregon coast, where many species of animals and plants depend upon its fragile, threatened environment; the same is true of Ironwood Forest in southern Arizona's Sonoran Desert.

There are only three law enforcement officers responsible for almost two million acres in the Grand Staircase-Escalante, and only one full-time archeologist. Call him Lew. He drives me onto the monument east of Kanab, unabashedly wearing his BLM T-shirt and speaking enthusiastically of the work he and other scientists—geologists, botanists, hydrologists, ecologists—do on the monument.

Entomologists have found forty species of bees on the lovely lavender bee weed lining the road. Paleontologists located unique fossilized dinosaur tracks on the ridge just west of us. "The breadth of research is one of the main pluses of preserving the monument. We can get universities and private individuals to put money in, and produce real science, unlike other BLM offices. We're lucky. But the current administration is important, and this one cares only for oil and gas."

He thrusts his GPS device out the window, to get his bearings. We pull over and hike through sagebrush to a site that was plundered years before but is still scattered with the dark shards from the Ancient Puebloan site, turned up by a bulldozer. "Here he put the [bulldozer] blade down and went right through," Lew says. "These used to be substantial masonry walls." More common these days are quick, discreet digs in places few people visit, by ATV-riding raiders who "find a little rock shelter and in an hour can destroy it."

At another site, he picks up a piece of pottery with three dots on it. "Basketmaker three," he says, referring to Basketmaker III, the stage of Pueblo culture that dates from approximately 500 to 700 A.D. "If we find a projectile point, it will be a tiny triangle with a small stem at the bottom." He will return to Kanab to record this site on the U.S. Geological Survey map, a process requiring a couple of hours' work, including filling out several forms.

We find stones marking the boundaries of what was a house with a storage unit; I would have passed it by without noticing. "This is late Kayenta," one of four types of the so-called Ancient Puebloans, toward the end of the occupation. They left roughly eight hundred years ago, for reasons still in dispute (drought perhaps, or warfare, or both). Three holes have been dug by pot hunters. "This is the midden where people, and pots, were buried. That's what they're after." The various cultures often buried their dead with utensils, tools, weapons, and clothing, all very valuable today.

We climb the side of a canyon and make a significant discovery of our own: prehistoric paintings of hunters and indecipherable symbols. Unfortunately, part of the wall is covered with propelled cow shit that has dried and hardened. "Cows like to shelter up here," Lew says. He has been trying to document the effect of grazing on cultural resources, and "this is a pretty good example of the problems we have managing this area."

The state BLM director's predecessor asked ranchers

to remove some cattle from the monument during drought and supported efforts by environmentalists to buy out the grazing rights. Some ranchers within the monument had agreed to sell their grazing rights if compensated by the Grand Canyon Trust, an action that would also have benefited cultural resources. She was transferred, and the BLM announced that it could open any lands to grazing it saw fit, even if those in possession of the rights didn't want to use them. When I ask the acting director about this, he says, "Grazing is a right, not a privilege." Nongrazing, he adds, is not a right.

We climb to another canyon wall, where granaries were built to store corn almost a millennium before, the handprint of a builder in red earth still clearly visible. The view is of a landscape where little prehistoric field houses once stood, surrounded by crops on the valley floor. Smoke would have risen in the evenings from many fires outside the houses on the flats and in the canyon walls, under an immense sky. "Imagine sitting here then," Lew says, "looking out over all this, listening to the corn rattle in the wind."

THE NATIONAL LANDSCAPE Conservation System is one of the most audacious visions for public lands in American history, one recognizing the commonality of large, if disparate, iconic spaces, and a sense of national well-being inherent in them. Bruce Babbitt told BLM employees in 2000, when the NLCS was created, that the agency could "set the standard for protecting landscapes . . . and bringing people together to live in harmony with the land. Or, it can become a relic."

Harmony hardly describes what is now taking place on BLM lands. The agency's political appointees throw up their hands in the enforcement battle and tacitly—never explicitly—acknowledge that the bureau is unequal to the task. Meanwhile, energy exploration and extraction, grazing, and offroading impose increasingly serious burdens. BLM spokespersons in the West and in Washington, D.C., blame the paucity of law enforcers or lack of funds, rather than priorities, implying that adequate protection would be afforded the land, and better lists of historic assets compiled, if only the agency had more money.

But when I later ask about the budget, I discover that the agency has plenty of money for management of, say, "fluid energy mineral/oil and gas" ($87 million). The total for energy and minerals is $107 million, grazing $69 million, recreation $44 million, and mining about $33 million. Out of one year's $3 billion BLM enchilada, law enforcement receives only $17 million—$22 million less than the wild horse and burro program—and cultural resources receive only $15 million.

Local jobs created by gas and oil extraction and mining disappear once the resources are exhausted, taking scenic beauty and good water with them. The beneficiary of these policies is corporate America, which generally pays unrealistically—and sometimes illegally—low fees. The BLM failed to raise the rate of royalties paid in 2005 by energy companies for natural gas taken from public lands, thus proudly depriving itself of $700 million, more than enough to pay for decades of real law enforcement, and rewarding the energy developers.

Secretary of Interior Gail Norton declined to discuss any of these topics before she abruptly quit, just one of many appointees to leave in disgrace due to favoritism, exploitation, incompetence, and worse. So did the BLM's director. Obtaining the opinion of anyone in authority at the Interior Department, or hard facts about money and priorities, involves a drawn-out, largely fruitless process of requests, issue "clarification," and official avoidance that's comical, cowardly, and sad, all at the same time. The director of the NLCS did agree to be interviewed, then canceled without explanation.

Many career BLM employees are dedicated to preserving the NLCS, and the neglect of cultural and natural assets remains a sore subject indeed within the agency. In 2005, a career employee and director of Carrizo Plain National Monument in California, in despair over the condition of public lands in her bailiwick, killed herself with a .38 caliber revolver. She was in charge of the 250,000 acres bisected by the San Andreas Fault, the largest surviving bit of the San Joaquin River grasslands, crucial habitat for unique species and part of the NLCS, and her attempts to limit grazing on the monument had been opposed by the usual alliance of ranchers and Interior officials.

The same year, the state of New Mexico, in a highly unusual move, charged in court that the BLM had failed to comply with the National Historic Preservation Act before allowing oil and gas development on Otero Mesa, part of the ecologically sensitive Chihuahuan Desert and scattered with some fifty thousand archaeological and historic sites. And a Montana district judge ruled that the BLM violated the National Historic Preservation Act for not negotiating in good faith with the Northern Cheyenne before allowing massive coal-bed methane gas development, using the word "misleading" to describe the agency's tactics, a diplomatic allusion to a culture of deception that still flourishes.

TWENTY YEARS AGO, during President Reagan's administration, I toured public lands in the West—mostly BLM lands, many of them now part of the National Landscape Conservation System—and wrote a book about the experience: *The Kingdom in the Country.* Development was aggressively pursued then, too, but without today's sophisticated blend of ideology, bumbling, and raw commerce in public property. Officially sanctioned "privatization," unrestrained exploitation of resources, failure to collect fees for them, and hiding from public inquiry are much worse today.

The BLM's history, like its current modus operandi, indicates that unlimited access to land, resource extraction, development, and grazing are absolute values. Those who want to conserve anything at all are considered the enemy. At this point, nothing could compel the BLM to do an adequate job of conservation, and therefore a draconian solution must be found. Perhaps a supra-agency could be created by congressional fiat to override the authority of the resource dispensers and gather the assets into a single basket—a kind of National Landscape Conservation Administration modeled on the Depression-era efforts. More likely would be a radical reshuffling of the BLM's management policies and a direct subsidy from Congress to ensure protection, but the chance of either possibility being realized in the current atmosphere of dishonesty and messianic free enterprise is nonexistent.

The original designation of vast communal lands in the West was a blessing for the country and an example for the world. Now the challenge is to preserve what's left of them. This will require an enlarging of the national perspective—figuratively and literally—and living landscapes are vital to this task. For at the moment, the nation denies itself nothing, including squandered resources requiring the abandonment of whole cultures and the destruction of the very ground upon which America was built.

Chapter 17

NAPA, MANIFEST DESTINATION

THE POOLSIDE POETRY READING WAS ORGANIZED by a slim, dark-haired woman whose family owns the sea of vineyard washing up at the patio's edge. Distant hills gold in the August sun, parched air, and shadows sharp as stilettos are familiar components of the valley of the Napa River, but this could as easily be Tuscany, or Provence, and as different from southeast Utah as it can be. Yet both share relentless demands that are transforming America, as well as the West.

The guests sitting on folding chairs and sipping sauvignon blanc, which is made from the fruit of these same vines, wear jeans or chinos, Bermudas or designer casual, and all of them clearly *belong*. Their lives are at least tangential to one of the most valuable legal crops in America. Growing grapes and making and selling wine, or its downstream bounty—real estate, promotion, investment—produce income for most of these people, and they are happy to contribute to the local arts on a Sunday afternoon before going off to Bistro Jeanty or Tra Vigne for dinner.

Less than one hundred yards from where they sit is a stone marker noting the settlement of Napa Valley by one George Calvert Yount, a peripatetic North Carolina trapper, rancher, and miller who in 1837 built an adobe house, long gone. The figurative distance between that commemorative stone and this contemporary scene is vast. The valley Yount first entered was almost Edenic: a redwood canopy on the western mountains that the sun rarely penetrated, streams running year-round and brimming with steelhead and salmon, grizzlies feeding upon them, and peaceable Wappo Indians soon to be extirpated by introduced disease and then outright slaughter. The lush valley floor would prove ideally suited to grazing and the growing of wheat. Yount, who would be granted the sprawling Caymus Ranch by the Mexican government, built a gristmill and sawmill and is credited with planting the first vine in Napa Valley. But it is a far cry from the vines producing the stylish chardonnays and cabernet sauvignons today.

Agriculture in some form has been a part of this place for at least a century and a half. The visual motif of farming is arguably more cultural than natural, and it once included fruit and nut orchards, vegetables in great variety, livestock, and cereals in addition to grapes. Napa Valley qualifies as a cultural landscape—meaning agriculture—and its survival in one of the most lucratively developable stretches in America seems increasingly a wonder, and an anomaly. Top-water farming and the heterogeneous community built around it, from pruner to mogul, were the things that drew me to the subject of Napa Valley two decades ago.

Demands upon American space are not new, but the land's apparent finiteness is. Here the domination by vines instead of cattle or other crops is fairly recent. Grapes are worth $400 million annually, but the total economic impact of wine is probably ten times that. Wine remains an adjunct of farming and is vital to the identity of a remarkable place whose preeminence in American viticulture is established. But the combination of money and fame has proven irresistible to forces destructive of both community and a landscape that has become an agricultural icon. How farming, and the life and landscape inherent in it, can be preserved in a discrete place celebrated not just for its product but also for its aesthetic value is still an open question.

Threats to the valley's identity include multimillionaires determined to have their own monumental houses and wineries, but also expanding cities, tourism, and corporate control of the land. Napa Valley, in its highly visible way, embodies many of the challenges found elsewhere in America, something I realized when I first visited Napa and found a seemingly alien substance—wine—that had given rise to its own land ethic. The

Napa County board of supervisors in 1968 had set a twenty-acre minimum lot size, which has since increased and has caused rancorous debate but would lead to the acceptance of agriculture as the best use of the land. It allowed the county to tax productive farmland according to its agricultural rather than its developmental value, thus ensuring that farmers—grape growers—could stay in business even as real estate boomed.

It was the first official "agricultural preserve" in America, and I was interested in writing about it and the people—primarily corporate and academic dropouts—who brought it about. They had acted on the old countercultural impulses of the 1960s, but by the 1980s, some of these people were getting rich. They were long-standing members of a subculture that most Americans didn't recognize—a world in which local newspapers ran stories about vintages and grape varieties and printed ads for bud wood and smudge pots. I was struck by its interrelatedness: jobs, grape deals, marriages, shared equipment, advice, and spats, all of it grounded in a devotion to grapes as well as wine. It was a community.

No more. In 1988, a fight developed between winery owners and grape growers over winery definitions, presaging fiercer environmental battles to come. Some in the valley wanted limitations on the number and size of what were no longer just boutique bottling operations, while others—primarily the big wineries—wanted no restrictions, since there were larger profits to be made from development and tourism. These new tensions enlivened a social landscape that already had a high annual population growth. One point of the book I wrote then—*Napa: The Story of an American Eden*—was that for special places to survive, those in control must make concessions to posterity.

In 1999, I returned to the valley and was surprised to see so many big, new houses and wineries, despite the limitations imposed, and to find the battles among the wineries, growers, and environmentalists more pitched and more uncompromising than before. The questions raised in the grower-winery fight a decade before had clearly not been resolved, and dot-commers and other newly rich had placed on the land hyperthyroid, choose-your-period mansions with baronial stone walls, giant lawn sculptures, and designer wineries.

Despite this, at the end of the twentieth century, Napa Valley was still an exemplar of natural beauty and opportunity, but also showed symptoms of the gigantism that has afflicted so many new American structures—the architectural and intellectual equivalent of obesity. The forested heights of the Howell and Mayacamas ranges on both sides of the valley were being scraped raw to provide vineyards for those desperate to have them at any cost, and the valley floor was notable for long lines of often stationary cars.

I wrote a second book—*The Far Side of Eden*—about these newcomers' impact in the valley, focusing on the fight over hillside vineyards and related development that affected the health of not just the river but also the carefully preserved landscape. The natural scenery had proven value for both citizens and visitors, but absentee homeownership of the sort that plagues many sought-after American places was now a problem for the valley as well, as were the loss of commonality and demands for services unrelated to the practice of agriculture.

Today, new architectural "statements," some made on ridgelines, continue to alter the valley's character. Increasingly, wineries advertise the artistic sensibilities of owners whose interest in wine is more social than viticultural. The pioneering spirit of the 1960s has been replaced by a desire for notoriety and a style of life unrelated to the land as anything more than a backdrop, and in many cases, the architecture is clearly more important than the wine. Function follows fashion.

The internationally known Swiss architects Herzog & de Meuron, for example, some years ago created a massive stone winery outside Yountville for Dominus Estates. The winery is visually stunning and totalitarian in aspect; it excludes visitors, including locals, and symbolizes the unapproachable "vintner" elite. And for a winery just south of St. Helena, architect Frank Gehry designed a structure that would swallow a smaller, historic stone winery built in 1885 by a New England sea captain and later owned by the Napa Valley Cooperative Winery, which in the 1930s and 1940s produced about half of all Napa Valley wines. Thus, a highly visible, contemporary structure reflective of fashion, not function, reduces the authentic and historically resonant to an ornament.

The objection of local residents to the new winery is that it will attract five hundred visitors a day for the wrong reason—spectacle. The paradox is that tourists want natural beauty but at the same time demand amusements and accommodations that make change inevitable. Tourism is now worth about $500 million a year to the county. "But tourism depends upon agriculture," says Jim Hickey, the county's former planning director, over a glass of chardonnay in the Bounty Hunter in the city of Napa, "and agriculture depends upon land. If you destroy ag, there's no reason for the tourist to come here."

It was Hickey who so famously said, back in the 1980s, "If Napa Valley can't be saved, no place can." The unique combination of natural assets, good laws, an extraordinarily valuable crop, and informed citizenry should have enabled Napa to withstand the more destructive demands of developers. Now, as Hickey points out, "everyone wants an increasingly larger piece of the tourist income. If we ever reach the point where tourism, not agriculture, drives the economy, we've lost the ballgame."

The most suitable land for development borders the proximate cities of Napa and American Canyon, a flourishing bedroom community, and the towns of Yountville, St. Helena, and Calistoga. The agricultural preserve still exists, but even farming protected by legislation can't support unlimited additions. And tourists and new householders like agriculture in the abstract but complain of the dust it raises, the noise made by farm machinery, the use of chemicals, and the grape-hauling gondolas that contribute to rural traffic jams.

That many winery owners push behind the scenes for changes in land-use regulations to allow them to expand further is an ugly irony, since it is they who should be protecting the status quo. It was the struggling winemakers who back in the 1960s got the agricultural preserve law through the local board of supervisors, but changes now proposed by the newer wineries would allow more parking lots and related enterprises capitalizing on tourism. Some wineries are tacit allies of developers and potential retailers who claim commercial rights in the countryside and argue that exceptions to the zoning laws are both necessary and inevitable.

To McMansions, winery expansions, and tourism is added another danger: large corporations, which own 20 percent of the valley's approximately forty-five thousand acres of vineyard and other real estate. Constellation Brands acquired what is perhaps the most potent symbol of Napa's phenomenal success, the Robert Mondavi Winery, a formerly family operation that is now a mere adjunct of a multinational based in upstate New York. Beringer, one of the oldest and most renowned names among historic Napa wineries, is owned by the Fosters Group, Australia's enormous beer-based conglomerate. Beaulieu Vineyard, established by Georges de Latour as a quality Gallic outpost here at the outset of the twentieth century, belongs to the gigantic English liquor distributors Diageo. Other sizable portions of land are held by companies in Switzerland, France, Italy, and Argentina.

Corporations are sometimes efficient mechanisms for producing revenue, but dreadful exemplars of social responsibility, since the ultimate objective is profits, not community or democracy, and the most single-minded rise at the expense of all else. Corporations do not pay inheritance taxes, as individual growers and winery owners do, and when the going gets rough—if the provisions of the agricultural preserve were to be altered because the wine business temporarily tanked, as it has in the past—corporate leaders, unlike private citizens, will do what is necessary to prosper economically, including selling off vineyards for commercial and residential development without a moment of real regret.

More than a century ago, the notion was widely promulgated that America's destiny was the spreading of its people across a seemingly inexhaustible country, without much attention paid to what would come after. Now it is abundantly clear that the land is exhaustible and that many citizens want what's left of the country preserved in a recognizable state. Today, those two visions collide on the outskirts of cities and towns, even in the heart of Napa's ag preserve—one developmental and blatantly show-biz, the other agricultural and historic.

The valley's challenge—like the country's—is no longer to spread the populace and new enterprises everywhere, but to mitigate them. To survive as a place, America must instill in citizens an awareness of the evanescent qualities we once knew and loved, and of the dangers of Manifest Destiny's hangover. Judging by what has transpired since the arrival of George Yount in 1837, that's the most daunting task.

Chapter 18

THE STATE OF UTOPIA

Yes, there is a place where old warehouses are recycled as condos and offices, streetcars efficiently trundle passengers between home and work, and people are polite. They have organized themselves into influential neighborhood groups, the mayor rides a bicycle to protest the hegemony of the automobile, and a developer sends his engineer to China to study feng shui. Known as the City of Roses, it has the largest urban park in the country, and a reasonably short trip takes drivers to the gorge of the Columbia River or across unspoiled landscapes to Mount Hood or the rocky Pacific coast.

The city is, of course, Portland, Oregon. I went there to learn how the concern with open space and quality of life had given the state a reputation as a place apart, and if communities were holding on to this reality; driving around, I experienced a pleasant sense of time past—no isolated strip malls in the countryside or dinky housing developments beyond community limits, and a more or less neat divide between urban and rural that is at odds with America's sprawling development ethic.

Oregon has lost about half as much rural land and open space as other states have lost. Of a total of sixty-two million acres of scenic landscape, half of it forested, more than seventeen million are in private ownership. In 2004, a shadow was cast across all this by a statewide referendum that turned people into adversaries and gave pause to community planners all across America. Known as Measure 37 and put forward by property rights advocates, it stated that government "must pay owners, or forego enforcement, when certain land use restrictions reduce property value" and passed with 61 percent of the vote. Persons or their heirs who owned property prior to 1973 and still owned it were to be granted waivers of the old laws. If not, they had to be compensated for any loss of value due to building restrictions.

Measure 37 became infamous—or righteous, depending upon your point of view. In effect, it created two classes of citizens: those bound by state and local building regulations and those free to do anything they pleased with their land and to prosper from it in ways their neighbors could not. It also threatened to undo—or undid—decades of practice that in effect kept Oregon whole for everyone coming after.

Basically an antigovernment vote, Measure 37 dealt a geopolitical shock to the state bureaucracy and promised to profoundly affect not just the rural communities and vistas for which the state is justly famous—and on which depends a seven-billion-dollar tourist trade—but the cities and suburbs as well. Oregon's long-standing land-use laws were the most sweeping statewide zoning requirements in the United States, and that prompted me, at least, to think that whatever happened to California, Montana, Virginia, or Nantucket, there would always be an Oregon.

Essentially antisprawl, those laws were passed in 1973 by a Democratic legislature and a moderate Republican, Tom McCall, a near-mythic governor who passionately believed in conservation. He worked with farmers and environmentalists, planners and local officials to gain passage of Senate Bill 100, which required all counties to plan for future development. Urban growth boundaries were established around cities, with development restrictions both inside and outside those boundaries. This prevented free-sprawling development and simultaneously preserved open space and urban cores by redirecting growth back into the cities.

From that cooperative time to present-day America, with its uncompromising attitudes about everything from regulation to religion, is a long journey indeed. The zoning restrictions worked well in Oregon for thirty years. Then, opponents put forward Measure 37 as a supposed savior of farmers and old people who couldn't cash out their properties, blaming the existence of the zoning restrictions on urbanites and stigmatizing Portland as a place of elitists. In fact, the measure was driven by timber operators, disgruntled rural residents whose land was never productive in the first place, and, of course, their proxies—right-wing ideologues with a general detestation of anyone opposed to their views on a wide range of subjects, from race to abortion.

All this is ironic, since Portland reflects values—democracy, responsibility, restraint—celebrated as all-American before the advent of the self-serving property rights orthodoxy. Portland may be countercultural but not in the Aquarian sense. There are bumper stickers saying "Wake me in 2008," "Keep Portland Weird," and "My other car is a broom," but civic lessons abound, from clean streets to accessible elected officials. The city remains the antithesis of flashier and considerably less livable boom towns like Seattle, Denver, and Dallas. Though a beneficiary of computer technology—Portland hasn't enjoyed the success of Washington's Redmond, home of Microsoft, or Silicon Valley to the south—the unemployment rate remains relatively high. But new, mostly young residents are drawn to an alternative style of metropolitan life not dominated by corporations, cars, and suburbs. The large influence of open space on this sensibility is one important story of the recent urban past.

"PORTLAND DIFFERS from other American cities," I'm told by a professor at Portland State University—wool tie, short hair, no beads, utilitarian desk—"because in the mid-sixties, activists took Jane Jacobs seriously." He's referring to Jacobs's book *The Death and Life of Great American Cities,* which advocates diversity of people and structures in cities. It champions historic preservation, street life, easily accessible urban cores, and small development projects as opposed to gargantuan ones—"an essential vision of what should matter."

Portland was hit by the same urban renewal that blighted other cities in the 1960s. Much of south Portland and the Albina district in the north and northeast were razed, as were many cast-iron facades throughout downtown. But the new plan of 1973, the professor adds, "was about human scale and pedestrian interaction at a time when cities were struggling with suburbs. The neighborhood movement provided strong identity for specific places, and a decision was made to favor access over outward mobility."

Progressive city officials and community members in 1975 killed a plan for a freeway that would have cleared a large swath in southeast Portland; the money was rechanneled into what eventually became an efficient light-rail system, and Portland joined outlying communities in a cooperative regional government. The decision to invest in public transport ultimately included a train that served the airport and helped reduce downtown traffic and air pollution.

This active engagement by citizens goes all the way back to settlement in the nineteenth century by families interested in community, in sharp contrast to Seattle and San Francisco, which grew out of predominantly male enterprises—timber, gold—fueled primarily by the desire for wealth. Portland resounds with the bells on sleek, Czech-designed trolleys and on bicycles that are not just tolerated but encouraged. Used bikes can be rented cheaply and are imaginatively recycled—in one case into a daiquiri blender, according to the *Oregonian*. People between twenty-four and thirty-five years of age, the so-called young creatives, are attracted to Portland in unusually high numbers, willing to work as baristas if it means they have time off for skiing or some other out-of-doors experience.

Easterners—and Californians—were attracted to Portland back in the 1960s and early 1970s by the existence of cheap, old houses that could be fixed up. In 1968, Portland adopted a preservation ordinance, and in 1975, the Historic Landmark Commission designated its first historic district—Skidmore/Old Town, which is in the National Historic Register. Since then, preservation has become a commodity in its own right. In the late 1960s, a young builder began buying the architectural gleanings of improvident destruction and selling them to what he calls countercultural pioneers. Today, he owns Rejuvenation, a thirty-million-a-year business, and sells the same thing to middle-class homeowners who are sometimes obsessive in their concern for authenticity and "turning their houses into museums."

Developers, often the villains, instead became involved in adaptive use in Portland. The local McMenamin brothers converted older buildings to new uses, including a school transformed into a brew pub (Terminator Stout, Hammerhead ale). Though it seemed counterintuitive, developers profited from the creation of the urban growth boundary because the city decided in 1991 to cut its lot sizes in half, increasing residential density, and to offer tax and other incentives for adaptations of existing structures that contained low-income housing and retail.

Old warehouses and factories in northwest Portland's Pearl district were converted into condos, a few with eighteen-foot windows and a price of more than a million dollars, "snapped up by cross-commuters who work in the suburbs and come back here to live," the man who developed it proudly tells me. "Now there are cooking classes and wine tastings, lots of clubs and things to do." He's only thirty-nine and has the slightly dazed look of the suddenly wealthy, having taken advantage of a state program allowing a fifteen-year freeze on taxes from properties listed on the National Register.

The Pearl is indeed alive with shops, cafés, and microbreweries; artists offer their work on scrubbed, cobbled streets that are jammed on First Thursday, the monthly appreciation day. (What's missing on these streets, as in so much of regentrified America, is children.) By redirecting business back into the city, the urban growth boundary contributed to urban contentedness, no small accomplishment. "The urban growth boundary protects the value of property within it and the quality of life," I'm told by a builder long involved with historic structures. "Those who develop farmland diminish everyone else's values."

Another maverick builder proposed developing the east side of the Willamette River not with staples like The Home Depot and Lowe's, big-box stores typically favored by his rivals, but with "green" structures for local businesses. He founded his business in a nearby rehabbed warehouse that now contains small-scale design and start-up firms and a fine restaurant with the droll name of Clark Lewis (serious Italian wine list, factory *vérité* in exposed ducts, concrete floor, and tattooed waitresses). Utilitarian chic extends to his boardroom and earth-toned shirt and tie. "Developers have gotten used to double-digit returns," he says, "but over-the-top profits come at the expense of the public. We need to incubate a creative economy that seeps into the urban core"—shades of Jane Jacobs.

But a philosophical shift in attitudes toward government regulation was detected in 2003, when an initiative similar to Measure 37 passed, only to be struck down in court on a technicality. A veteran preservationist later explains that it targeted preservation instead of rural land and was known as the owner consent law. It shifted from mandatory to voluntary decisions to preserve historic properties by allowing owners to remove them from the state's official list. "It was just a matter of time until the property-rights types moved on to the next resource."

Opposition to Measure 37 was led in part by the non-profit 1000 Friends of Oregon, founded in 1975. At that time, staff attorneys resolved conflicts between landowners and local boards, and the group helped correct misinterpretations of the law, became the most influential conservation group in a state full of them, and, over the years, helped build a political majority for good land use. Meanwhile, the urban growth boundary in effect deregulated the housing market inside it. The connection between rural conservation and investment in the cities wasn't lost on the developers of low-end housing, who saw green space as a boon.

So it came as a surprise in 2004 that, with $2.8 million to spend, the campaign of 1000 Friends of Oregon against Measure 37 failed, although property-rights advocates had a lot less money. "They knocked our lights out," says a cofounder of 1000 Friends, sitting in northwest Portland's Boulangerie one rainy morning, over good coffee, a must in this city. "They put a ninety-two-year-old widow on television who said she was losing everything. Voters didn't mean to screw up land use; they were just reacting to the ads."

According to 1000 Friends' executive director, "people didn't believe the land was threatened. The proponents of Measure 37 focused on a few seemingly sad stories. They cast it as fairness and compensation." Five months after passage, about 250 property-rights claims had been made in Oregon. A month later, there were about 400, and in less than a year, more than 1,000.

The big question remained: Were waivers to existing zoning regulations transferable to buyers of the properties in question? "The landowners can subdivide," I was told by the director of the Department of Land Conservation and Development in Salem, the state capital, "but the lots themselves are still subject to the former regulations." One local court case was brought to determine whether these new "rights" could be passed on to second buyers, but ultimate authority rested with the state legislature, which didn't act.

Most of the claimants under Measure 37 would have to be granted the right to develop protected lands because state and local governments can't afford to pay compensation. Thus, the vote introduced the unknown into planning on all levels and indirectly affected many decisions concerning property. In Portland proper, plans for a wildlife conservation program based upon a requirement that property owners preserve habitat were scuttled; dozens of claims under Measure 37 were filed for compensation for planned development that was denied because of the city's existing environmental regulations. In short, the aftermath of the law was potentially disastrous for the countryside, and for the city.

FIFTEEN MILES FROM downtown Portland, the new office complexes and sales emporiums abruptly end; the traveler can still enter what the state preservation officer calls "a time warp out of Knott's Berry Farm," meaning green fields, trees, orchards, little farmhouses, and overall a sense of purpose and repose. I wonder, seeing it for the first time, how even the most determined property-rights advocates would want to alter it, and decide to ask.

Oregonians in Action (OIA) is located in the suburb of Tigard, just south of Portland, inside the urban growth boundary. Malls alternate with prefab warehouses, service centers, and ugly, tilt-up, low-rise office buildings. OIA's utilitarian headquarters in one of them has lots of promotional handouts and workers who scrutinize the visitor to see if he really belongs here; I'm finally escorted to the office of a heavyset young man in an open shirt.

An integral part of the organization, he throws himself back in his chair to savor OIA's victory. "We're the largest property-rights group in the country," he says proudly. "Our goal is to direct development and protect the most valuable land."

By that he means farms. He would do it in a unique way—by allowing more houses to be added to farm-steads, "to stop their decline. Residential development doesn't harm farming. And if the farmer doesn't want people next door, let him buy the property."

I get the impression that he thinks subdivision is good stewardship of the land. I decide not to point out the absurdity of this and instead mention that the sudden creation of wealth for long-term property owners under Measure 37 will cause an equal drop in the value of their neighbors' land. He claims property owners have been treated unequally since the 1970s, when Senate Bill 100 was implemented, and that agricultural communities in arid, hardscrabble eastern Oregon need help. This is in part true, and almost totally irrelevant. Most suc-cessful Oregon farmers opposed Measure 37 because it would flood farmland with houses. Its major support came not from farmers—or developers. "Trying to get money out of a developer," he says, "is like trying to get blood from a stone." No, it came from those embittered hardscrabblers in eastern Oregon and from holders of large tracts of land on which stand Oregon's signature "crop," trees.

Oregonians in Action seems opposed to all restric-tions on individual gain involving property, regardless of the social impact, and in favor of a bleak world in which local agencies or the courts, not the state, arbitrate protracted fights among neighbors over compensation and quality of life. I detect what sounds like contempt in his words and in the literature spread around the office. He purports not to oppose land-use planning in general, but "in Oregon they don't plan for where people live, but for how they live. We may have a land-use system unlike any in the country, but it's not a model, because it doesn't work."

Of course, it has worked, and worked well for decades, as evidenced by the urban growth boundaries and the state's relatively healthy environment for life as well as business. But of Portland's prize Pearl district, he says, "You have to give people tax breaks to move there. It will be a ghetto in ten years." With now palpable resentment, he blames people in the cities for unduly influencing state legislators, particularly those in Portland. Finally I get it: This is a double issue—part envy, part class—resonating around the country wherever people feel out of control of their lives and fortunes and attack their own sensible zoning laws, rather than corporations, corrupt pols, and wealthy individuals whose self-interest has hurt them.

Meanwhile, property-rights groups are inviting this young lawyer to advise them in their struggle against urbanites who glory in unspoiled, what he calls "free" landscapes. These spoiled urbanites "drive through them in their Saabs," he says—later it becomes Volvos with the tops down—"and don't want their visual sensibilities disturbed." He drops his guard completely. "They don't want to look at two houses on a lot outside the city, he says, jerking a thumb at his unlovely vista, "but they want me to look at them."

LAND-USE RESTRICTIONS in some form have existed in America since the time of the Continental Congress; if the free market was the only consideration in Portland, there would be no revitalized Pearl, no Pioneer Courthouse Square, no riverfront park, no light rail, and elsewhere no beach or view protection. Most of the preserved structures would not have survived, nor would farms and historic sites as Oregonians know them.

The state is the largest U.S. producer of grass seed, Christmas trees, berries, peppermint, and hazelnuts, and a ranking supplier of such disparate commodities as hops, cauliflower, and nursery products. A $4 billion industry, farming accounts for one in twelve jobs. The Willamette Valley south of Portland is the foremost producer of grass seed in the world and a premier growing region for other crops, including fine pinot noir grapes.

Outside the town of McMinnville, I find Gary Johnson, a fourth-generation farmer, fertilizing his perennial rye grass in a thirty-acre field next to a filbert orchard; we talk in his pickup, out of the rain. "If they dump more people in the agricultural area," he asks, "who gets hurt? I could put fifteen houses here, but then I couldn't do anything else with it. You've used up the natural resource."

He disagrees with the assertion that subdivisions don't affect farming. There are already some commuters in the neighborhood, and Johnson receives complaints from them regularly—that his water truck spoils the view, that his sheep smell. I am reminded of wealthy dot-commers in Napa Valley complaining of dust stirred up by grape gondolas hauling the raw product that goes into the product that produces the cachet they bought into in the first place. Multiply those complainers by ten, and soon, adverse political pressure is brought to bear on agriculture. The state Farm Bureau foresaw this, but its board was evenly split over Measure 37 and so the organization took no official position on it.

The potential economic bonanza for people like Johnson remains great: "If they start compensating people, I guess I'll have to raise my hand like every other whore. Otherwise, you're denying opportunity." A lifelong Republican, he believes "some discreet change was necessary, but this is radical. We've had one of the most conservative, well-run farming communities anywhere," and now all is in doubt.

Just across the road from Johnson's field is a parcel of one hundred family-owned acres on which one hundred houses could theoretically have been put. "Some of my friends voted for Measure 37," Johnson says, "and they're sorry they did."

One draconian strategy discussed by opponents of Measure 37 inside the state bureaucracy is to allow some effects of the new law to play out. Then, voters across the state will begin to see the damage possible— wrecked rural landscapes, towering landfills, "a portfolio of horrors," as one official put it. Yet, within two years, there were more than two thousand claims on the state to either put up money or get out of the way of zoning violations, some of them gargantuan. The courts did not throw out Measure 37, and the politicians were not

about to go after a law with so many original supporters, although so many of them had since renounced it.
Court challenges continued—OIA's fond vision—over
the transferability of those new "rights."

Instead of trying to rally the public, 1000 Friends of
Oregon opted for legal "containment" of the damage; a
vacuum had developed in the environmental sphere in
a state where such a thing would have seemed impossible not so long ago.

Portlanders, too, wait for the Measure 37 shoe to
drop. "Here you're at the end of the country," says one
longtime community activist. "You can't afford San Francisco or Seattle—this is it. And there's an undercurrent
of anxiety that we are losing the things that made this
place special."

Portland's grassroots preservationists are often joined
by land-use advocates who have common interests in
preventing overdevelopment and face the same hurdles,
such as lack of public funds, a decline in the power of
the neighborhood organizations, and ironically, the city's
famous comity. "Being nice sometimes makes it hard to
get things done. Some of our successes happened a long
time ago. The whole city and the conservation movement need to have a conversation about what really
matters."

It seems to me that Measure 37 has forced such a
conversation. Citizens realize that the bloom on the City
of Roses isn't perennial, but so far it is just a conversation among the already converted; those opposed to any
restrictions aren't even listening. They are abetted by
political activists from elsewhere, some as distant as

the Manhattan real estate developer pumping money into Oregon and other states. My impression is that the property rightists would welcome a ghetto in the Pearl and elsewhere in Portland because it would justify their resentments of Volvo drivers and free landscapes.

Toward the end of my stay, a young creative says to me, in Stumptown, *the* café, "Utopias require peace of mind. There's a threat at our borders."

Downstream of the conjunction of the Willamette and the Columbia, the river takes on a broad, wild aspect. I decide to follow it to the mouth, crossing to Washington State near the port of Astoria. Thousands of logs are stacked like proverbial toothpicks, bounty of the hinterland, and beyond the broad sweep of water is neither river nor ocean, but a rich marriage of the two.

I stand on the westernmost point of land. Known as Cape Disappointment, the site named by the British explorer John Meares in 1788 after he failed to find a passage through the sandbar for his ship. (That honor went to the American fur trader Captain Robert Gray four years later.) Out there, the river contains no hint of its splendid origins, long passage, or Portland's travails. As in every American estuary, the troubling distillation of contemporary life is linked, but unresolved, in salty immensity. It was here that Lewis and Clark ended their historic westward perambulation amid damp ferns and towering hemlocks, the dark branches sheathed in moss and outstretched to the advancing fog.